ISBN 978-1-334-11118-1
PIBN 10562920

This book is a reproduction of an important historical work. Forgotten Books uses state-of-the-art technology to digitally reconstruct the work, preserving the original format whilst repairing imperfections present in the aged copy. In rare cases, an imperfection in the original, such as a blemish or missing page, may be replicated in our edition. We do, however, repair the vast majority of imperfections successfully; any imperfections that remain are intentionally left to preserve the state of such historical works.

English
Français
Deutsche
Italiano
Español
Português

www.forgottenbooks.com

Mythology Photography **Fiction**
Fishing Christianity **Art** Cooking
Essays Buddhism Freemasonry
Medicine **Biology** Music **Ancient
Egypt** Evolution Carpentry Physics
Dance Geology **Mathematics** Fitness
Shakespeare **Folklore** Yoga Marketing
Confidence Immortality Biographies
Poetry **Psychology** Witchcraft
Electronics Chemistry History **Law**
Accounting **Philosophy** Anthropology
Alchemy Drama Quantum Mechanics
Atheism Sexual Health **Ancient History**
Entrepreneurship Languages Sport
Paleontology Needlework Islam
Metaphysics Investment Archaeology
Parenting Statistics Criminology
Motivational

AUTHOR:

ORLEANS, CHARLOTTE-ELIZABETH

TITLE:

LIFE AND LETTERS OF CHARLOTTE...

PLACE:

LONDON

DATE:

1889

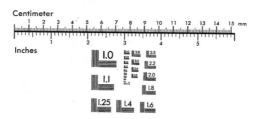

Centimeter

Inches

1.0 2.8 2.5
     3.2 2.2
     3.6
1.1   2.0

1.25 1.4 1.6 1.8

MANUFACTURED TO AIIM STANDARDS
BY APPLIED IMAGE, INC.

LIFE AND LETTERS
OF
CHARLOTTE ELIZABETH,
MOTHER OF PHILIPPE D'ORLEANS.

JAMES I. of ENGLAND

Frederick V.═Elizabeth Stuart

Electress Sophia   Karl Ludwig

George I.   CHARLOTTE ELIZABETH.

Elizabeth Charlotte
(Duchesse)
Palatine du Rhin
d'Orleans

LIFE AND LETTERS

OF

CHARLOTTE ELIZABETH

PRINCESS PALATINE

AND

MOTHER OF PHILIPPE D'ORLEANS, REGENT OF FRANCE

1652—1722

Compiled, Translated, and Gathered from various Published and
Unpublished Sources,

COMPRISING

THE ARCHIVES OF THE FRENCH FOREIGN OFFICE,
THE ARCHIVES OF THE HOUSE OF FRANCE, AND THE MANUSCRIPTS
IN THE BIBLIOTHÈQUE NATIONALE, PARIS.

LONDON: CHAPMAN AND HALL,
LIMITED,
1889.

PREFACE.

CHARLOTTE ELIZABETH was the eldest child of the Elector Palatine Karl Ludwig, and of Charlotte of Hesse Cassel, his wife. She was born in the Castle of Heidelburg on the 7th of July, 1652.

Married, on the 16th of November, 1672, to Monsieur, Philippe d'Orléans, Louis the Fourteenth's only brother. By him she had three children:— the Duc de Valois, born 1673—died 1676; the Duc de Chartres, who afterwards became the Regent, born 1674—died 1723; the Duchesse de Chartres, born 1676 — married to the Duc de Lorraine 1698—died 1744.

Charlotte Elizabeth's official title at the Court of Louis the Fourteenth was *Madame, Duchesse d'Orléans,* but she was generally styled MADAME by her contemporaries, whilst historically she is known as "the Princess Palatine, mother of the Regent."

She died on the 8th of December, 1722.

A selection of her letters, addressed to the Duke of Brunswick and Caroline of Anspach, then

Princess of Wales, were first published by Viewieg, at Brunswick, in 1789. A French translation, published by Maradou, attracted considerable attention in Paris. Another and somewhat fuller selection appeared in 1807. Since then divers collections and translations of parts of Madame's truly enormous correspondence have been brought out both in France and Germany, generally styling themselves, "Complete and Unabridged Correspondence of Charlotte Elizabeth, etc."

This, on the face of it, is clearly an impossible and absurd assertion, for the Princess Palatine is known to have written hundreds of letters to every Court in Europe. Many of her letters, specially those addressed to her German relations, never reached those to whom they were written, having been stopped at the frontiers as containing compromising political news of France. Others were probably destroyed on the death of the recipients, and many must even now be lying buried in the national archives of Spain, Savoy, Austria, and Italy, without speaking of what must have become of the long epistles Madame wrote to her friends in the French provinces, and to every small German principality. Till comparatively lately it was surmised that Madame's letters to her aunt, the Electress Sophia, had been destroyed by George I., who greatly disliked his cousin, but fortunately a volume of them was found and permission obtained to publish a selection of them.

Among Madame's correspondents were the Electress Sophia, her father's sister; her two step-daughters, the Queens of Spain and Sardinia; the Duchess of Modena; the Queen of Prussia, her first cousin; Mme. Von Harling, her old governess; and, later in life, Leibnitz, the famous German savant; the Raugravine Louise, her half-sister; her own daughter, the Duchesse of Lorraine and Bar; and Caroline of Anspach, at that time Princess of Wales. She wrote a large clear hand, and often spelt, both in German and French, the same word in five different ways. Keenly alive to the laws of courtesy and etiquette, her letters begin and end with innumerable protestations of friendship, respect, and assurances of her affection. Writing to her inferiors in rank, she generally signed herself, " your faithful friend, Charlotte Elizabeth."

Her letters reflect the life, not only of the Court of France, but of the English, German, and Spanish Courts of her time, and of the society which composed them. They also gave a vivid picture of the religious world, both Huguenot, Philosophical, and Roman Catholic.

We cannot do better than refer the reader to the account written of Madame by one of her contemporaries, the Duc de Saint Simon, and to the few admirably chosen words in which Mr. Thackeray sums up her personality and character. Saint Simon says : "*Madame tenait beaucoup plus de l'homme que de la femme, elle était forte cou-*

rageuse, Allemande au dernier point, franche, droite, bonne, bienfaisante, noble et grande en toutes ses manières; petite au dernier point sur tout ce qui regardait ce qui lui était dû. Elle était sauvage, toujours enfermée à écrire; dure, rude, se prenant aisément d'aversion. . . . . Capable avec cela d'une amitié tendre et inviolable. . , . ." And Thackeray, in the first chapter of his *History of the Four Georges:* " A woman whose honest heart was always with her friends and dear old Deutschland, though her fat little body was con. fined at Paris, Marly, or Versailles. . . . ."

MAY, 1889.

LIFE AND LETTERS

OF

CHARLOTTE ELIZABETH,

MADAME, MOTHER OF THE REGENT PHILIPPE D'ORLÉANS.

CHAPTER I.

1652 TO 1686.

To arrive at a just conception of Charlotte Elizabeth's character, it is necessary to understand from whence she derived her peculiar and strongly-marked individualities.

Her father, Karl Ludwig, was the second son of Frederick V., Elector Palatine and sometime King of Bohemia, and Elizabeth Stuart, daughter of James I.

Frederick V.'s strange mixture of weakness and combativeness, aided by his wife's ambition, involved him in the Thirty Years War, and destroyed the Palatinate, which was ravaged by Spinola and his Spanish troops.

The then Elector's children went out into the world to seek their fortune: among them was Prince Rupert, the well-known admiral and general under Charles I.

B

At the Peace of Westphalia a new Electorate was created in favour of Karl Ludwig, to whom the Palatine States were delivered over. He immediately set to work to bring back prosperity and wealth to the Palatinate; and succeeded so well that soon he became known as *the Regenerator*.[*] He had begun by recalling the families who had emigrated to Holland, England, and the neighbouring German states; and rebuilt Heidelburg Castle, which had fallen into a frightful state of ruin and neglect during the Thirty Years War. The new Elector also issued decrees that any one who restored one of the old town-houses in Manheim or Heidelburg should be freed from all taxation for two years; those who built new houses were exempt for three years, and those who planted vineyards for six years.

The University of Heidelburg, founded in 1386 by the Elector Ruprecht I., one of the oldest centres of learning in Germany, had also gone completely down during the Thirty Years War, and its splendid library was scattered to the four corners of the earth. Karl Ludwig reconstituted it as far as he was able, and Heidelburg became once again celebrated for its learning. Amongst those whom the Elector called to his aid was Spinoza, the great Jewish philosopher and metaphysician.

As religious differences had greatly contributed to the disasters which had fallen upon his states,

* Wiederhersteller.

he practised unlimited tolerance. The Calvinists were recalled, Roman Catholics and Lutherans dwelt in peace together, and even the Anabaptists arrived from Holland and formed themselves into a community at Manheim, where some of their descendants are now highly-respected citizens.

There exists a fine portrait of Madame's father, by Van Dyke, which shows the Elector as a powerful-looking man in the prime of life, his wonderfully-handsome countenance strongly resembling that of his mother, the unhappy Queen of Bohemia, whose beauty won her the title of the Queen of Hearts.

Having stated the excellencies of Karl Ludwig as a ruler, we must now turn to his private character as a man. He married on the 12th of February, 1650, Princess Charlotte of Hesse Cassel, a strange reserved woman, passionately fond of hunting and every sort of outdoor amusement, and quite indifferent to her husband's life and interests. Their quarrels began during the honeymoon.

Charlotte Elizabeth was born on the 7th of September, 1652, in the Castle of Heidelburg. Her infancy and childhood were passed amidst the constant quarrels of her father and mother, for shortly after Charlotte Elizabeth's birth the Elector fell violently in love with a certain Maria Susanna Louisa von Degenfeld, a beautiful girl of eighteen, and his own wife's maid of honour. His correspondence with the lady, which has been preserved, is extremely curious. Evidently finding

some difficulty in expressing his sentiments by
writing, he simply copied, almost word for word,
the love-letters contained in a romance which dealt
of the loves of a certain Lucretia, whose knight
wrote her long and passionate epistles in Latin.

Louise von Degenfeld's answers, although couched
in indifferent Latin, show a far brighter wit than do
the letters of her royal lover, or rather than those
he borrowed from Lucretia's knight.

This Fraulein von Degenfeld, who was destined
to play such an important part in Charlotte Elizabeth's history, does not seem to have been possessed
of the commonest principles of honour. She began
by showing Karl Ludwig's letters to the Electress,
and when the latter, greatly incensed, upbraided her
husband, the young maid of honour seemed to wish
to play the part of peacemaker, though keeping up
a secret correspondence meanwhile with the Elector.

After some time the Electress began to suspect
the truth; waiting for a favourable occasion to
publicly reproach the Elector, she invited one of her
brothers to come and see her, and in the middle of
a great banquet given in his honour she suddenly
disclosed to him her griefs and boxed her husband's
ears. After this things went from bad to worse till
1657, when the Elector applied for a divorce, which
was granted after some hesitation by the Diet of
Ratisbonne on the 17th of April, 1657.

Till the divorce had been actually notified to
her, Charlotte of Hesse Cassel does not seem to

have realised her position, but to have gone on
hunting, driving, and leading a solitary life, seeing
little of her children, and indifferent to her
husband's way of life. But we hear of her writing the Elector a letter almost immediately after
the divorce had been pronounced, which ended
with these words, "This is from the most ill-
used princess in Christendom, Charlotte, legitimate
Electress Palatine."

Her relations advised her to appeal to the Emperor, who, as lord of Germany, had a right to
interfere, but he refused to do anything for her,
and would only counsel her to go back to Heidelburg and live there quietly with her three children
as though nothing untoward had occurred.

This she made up her mind to do, but in the meantime the Elector had married Louise von Degenfeld,
and refused to allow his late wife access to her children unless she would promise to live on good terms
with her supplanter. This the unhappy Charlotte
of Hesse Cassel agreed to do, but her fortitude
gave way after a short time, and resolving on one
last effort she placed herself, "soberly dressed,
though not in widow's weeds," close to where the
Elector and his new wife were to pass in to supper.
We are told that she held the little Charlotte
Elizabeth by the hand, having bade her cry with
all her strength when she saw her father approach,
"Mercy! Mercy!"

When the Elector came forward Charlotte of

Hesse Cassel threw herself at his feet, begging him
to have pity upon her, and, if only for the sake of
their children and the probable effect on the succession, to recognise her for his lawful wife. The
Elector seemed greatly troubled and half turned
towards her, but Louise von Degenfeld murmured,
" Remember your promises to me," and drew him
away. Then Charlotte of Hesse Cassel hurried to
her own apartments, and took up a pistol, intending
to shoot her rival as she sat at supper, but Count
Hohenlohe, one of the Elector's gentlemen, sus-
pecting her intention, snatched it out of her hand
and called his master.

After this last appeal to her husband the Electress
entirely disappeared from Court, and was never
spoken of. Charlotte Elizabeth seems to have quite
forgotten her mother, who lived on a sad and solitary existence till death relieved her of her life.

Karl Ludwig lived with Louise von Degenfeld for
over twenty years. They had thirteen children,
in whose favour the Elector revived the old title of
Margrave and Margravine Palatines. To these half-
brothers and sisters Charlotte Elizabeth became
and remained warmly attached, remarking quaintly
in more than one of her letters to them : " It is not
your fault that we did not have the same mother."

When Louise von Degenfeld died * the Elector
was inconsolable, and spoke of his loss in piteous

---

* On the 18th of March, 1673.

---

terms to his sister the Electress Sophia of Hanover,
with whom he kept up a constant correspondence.
He wrote a curious account of "his beloved
Louise," celebrating her manifold virtues, her
beauty, cleanliness, intelligence, etc., but having
thus praised her good qualities he says that he is
bound to recall that "she did not always follow my
advice, and often saddened me by her ill-temper
and melancholy. But I am consoled," adds the
worthy Elector, "by the thought that during her
last illness neither care, nor physic, was spared to
make her well again."

Charlotte Elizabeth's first governess was a certain
Fraulein Offeln, to whom she became much
attached. One of the earliest letters known to
have been written by Madame is addressed to this
lady, and dated Amsterdam, March 9th, 1661, when
the Princess was only nine years old, and in which
she tells her that she often thinks of her, has had a
pleasant journey, and only complains of the way in
which the gnats have bitten her.

We know comparatively little of Charlotte
Elizabeth's early youth excepting through the
constant references in her after letters to the
dear old town of Heidelburg, the woods above
the castle, the town catechism, the simple fare,
and her happy, careless youth. She was brought
up till she was twelve years old by the Electress
Sophia, her father's sister, and in 1661 spent
some months in Holland. It was during this

sojourn in Amsterdam that she became acquainted with William of Orange.

Once the Elector gave Charlotte Elizabeth two hundred florins as a Christmas-box; a present never renewed, for Karl Ludwig was a careful man, and was not ashamed of the fact. His household expenses were not based on the number of persons, but of appetites which had to be provided for, less being given to those known to care but little for food.

A letter addressed to Madame von Harling,* Charlotte Elizabeth's late governess, gives us a glimpse of the life led by the Princess at the age of eighteen, shortly before the proposition of marriage with Monsieur:

"March 4th, 1670.

"I ought to tell you, dear Madame Harling, that my brother Charles † and myself had intended to disguise ourelves for Shrove Tuesday as gods and goddesses, but as the weather proved to be too cold the *fête* was put off, and yesterday was the day chosen. Our costumes were quite ready, and very handsome; my brother was to represent Mercury, and I, Aurora; Fraulein Kolb being Ceres, and another young lady Diana; there were also many shepherds and nymphs. The triumphal

* Mdlle. von Offeln married M. de Harling in 1669. Madame kept up an active correspondence in her after-life with both husband and wife.

† Charlotte Elizabeth's half-brother.

chariots were splendid. Just as we were going to begin arrived the news of the king of Denmark's death. We had to put everything off for six weeks, hoping that nothing else will occur in the interval. You must allow, dear Madame Harling, that your getting up early entirely depends on me, for am I not Aurora, and have I not the gate of the morn under my charge? Be sure that I shall only open them at the hour which suits me!"

Notwithstanding the Elector's scandalous behaviour to her mother, and his many oddities, Charlotte Elizabeth seemed to have heartily loved and admired her father, and she submitted to her fate without a murmur when told that she must leave her home, and the younger brothers and sisters to whom she had become so much attached, to be the second wife of Philippe d'Orléans, the King of France's only brother, Monsieur, the widower of the beautiful Henrietta of England, whose mysterious death by poison had been discussed by every Court in Europe, including, we may be sure, that of the Elector Palatine.

Charlotte Elizabeth gave in with a good grace to what was after all one of the clearest *mariages de convenances* the world has ever known. Owing to Louise von Degenfeld being but a morganatic wife, Charlotte Elizabeth presently remained the Elector's only legitimate child. By her marriage to his brother, Louis XIV. secured a principal right to the Palatinate and Bavaria. On the other hand, Karl

Ludwig was extremely glad to marry his daughter to the King of France's only brother.

Notwithstanding the Elector's liberal views, religious dissensions were still the order of the day in the Palatinate, and the Protestants felt keenly their young Princess's change of religion, though it is probable that the Electress Sophia's pupil held anything but Calvinistic views.

We are told that a Jesuit Père Jourdin was sent from Paris to assure himself of the bride's orthodoxy, for a certain Urbain Chevreau, believing that he would please the French Court, had already attempted to convert the young princess to the Roman Catholic religion. Curiously enough she had been neither brought up Calvinist nor Lutheran, but a mixture of the two, which resolved itself into something resembling the French Reformed Faith, or that held by the Huguenots.

When all was settled Charlotte Elizabeth bade good-bye for ever to her beloved Heidelburg and was brought by her father to Strasbourg, where she was delivered up into the hands of Anne of Gonsaga, who had been sent from Paris to meet her and send a description of the young German girl to her future home. As Anne of Gonsaga was Charlotte Elizabeth's own aunt, we may suppose that the *rapport* was not unfavourable. In exchange for the bride, Monsieur gave the Elector a receipt for 32,000 German florins, which constituted her dowry.

with blue enamel, contained in a gold case studded with turquoises and small diamonds. Two other watches, plain gold, contained in black chagreen cases studded with small gold nails."

Among her ornaments, the new Madame could show one object which was only fair to look upon, not useful; this was a little gold Cupid, studded all over with small rubies, diamonds, and pearls. Monsieur settled on her the Chateau of Montargis as her dower-house in case of his death; she afterwards constantly refers to Montargis with the dread of being exiled there both before and after Monsieur's death. This old chateau had been sold to Louis XIV. by the Duc de Guise, who had allowed it to fall into a half-ruined condition; and when it was settled on Madame her father never took the trouble to find out in what state the castle was, in which was to be his daughter's probable home in case of her becoming a widow. But the Elector's conduct with regard to the marriage-contract was far more culpable, for it left Madame penniless in case her husband happened to die before the birth of her child, or if she became a childless widow. Among the curious stipulations in the contract was one that Monsieur reserved the right of wearing all his late wife's jewels and ornaments.

Again, that anything Charlotte Elizabeth brought with her from Heidelburg would become half her husband's property. And that in case of her death he should appropriate all her jewels, gems, rings, bracelets, precious stones and ribbons; using many kinds of perfume and cosmetic. He was even said to rouge himself ! "

Madame also mentions in more than one of her letters her husband's love for rouge, and he always applied it to her cheeks himself whenever she would suffer it.

Although speaking French very imperfectly, knowing little or nothing of the family into which she had married, Madame immediately became Somebody, who must be considered, watched, consulted, and feared, both as being the first lady in the kingdom after the queen, and because of her own marked individuality.

She succeeded to the title, honours, and perils which had been borne by Henrietta of England, a graceful and melancholy figure who flitted through Louis XIV.'s brilliant Court, leaving the awful suspicion on her husband of having connived at her sudden death. And we are made to feel by the Court chronicles that all stood looking on with a certain interest and cold curiosity at the drama in which they believed the second Madame must also necessarily play the part of victim.

But soon it became clear to the onlookers that this Madame was made of sterner stuff than Charles L's unhappy daughter, and had her own ideas on every possible subject. Louis XIV., "Our Great Man," as she constantly designates him in her letters, was the only person powerful enough to

Louis XIV. esteemed highly her virtue, loyalty, and rough sincerity. He also sympathised with her love of outdoor life, dogs, horses, and the chase. The King never approved of her lonely and reserved way of life. When not occupied in hunting or going to the play she wrote long letters to her noble German relatives."

When Madame arrived in France Louis XIV. had just decided on making the château of Versailles one of his official residences, and a great part of Monsieur's life was necessarily spent with his brother, although Saint Cloud was supposed to be his own peculiar property. Madame's whole life was therefore passed in the small though beautiful belt of country near Paris in which Versailles, Saint Cloud, Marly, and St. Germains are situated. We hear of her living sometimes at Fontainebleau, and often in Paris, but most of her letters are dated from Versailles.

Like her mother, Charlotte of Hesse Cassel, Madame became passionately fond of hunting. Her father had never allowed her to learn riding, and she tells us that she must have had at least twenty tumbles before she learnt to stick on properly. As Louis XIV. hunted several times a week Madame was able often to enjoy her favourite diversion in the beautiful woods of Marly, St. Germains (where lived James II. and Mary of Modena), and the forest of Le Vesinet.

In the following passage of a letter addressed to

the Electress Sophia, Madame gives a touching account of her grief when leaving her father at Strasbourg:

To the Electress Sophia.

"Saint Germain, Feb. 3rd, 1672.

"Madame de Wurtemburg spoke the truth when she described my grief to Dorndorff. I cried all night from Strasbourg to Châlons. I showed myself far more indifferent than I really was in feeling. I cannot forgive myself for the manner with which I parted from my relatives in Strasbourg.

"I will tell you one thing about Monsieur: he is the best man in the world, and we get on very well together. None of his portraits resembled him in the least."

By this we see that the second Madame instinctively upheld her husband, and through all her letters during his lifetime she constantly mentions him with praise and a certain affection, as contrasted to his evil councillors and those about the Court.

Madame, through her marriage to Monsieur, became step-mother to Henrietta of England's daughters, whom she entirely adopted as her own children, taking great pains with their education, and caring after their health. But early in the year 1673 Madame's eldest child was born, and the title of Duke de Valois given him by Louis XIV., to her great satisfaction, for Madame held to etiquette and the honour she considered due to her rank with all the strength of her German nature.

c

To MADAME VON HARLING.

"July 6th, 1673.

"I often think of the joy you must have felt on being told of my safe deliverance of a boy. As I have always been like your own child it is as though you had heard of the birth of a grandson. I feel sure that he has your heartiest good wishes. As soon as he has had his portrait taken I will send it to you; but I hope that you will see him some day and find him all that you could wish. Thank God he is a fine and healthy child, and has been so since the day of his birth. His size and beauty give me great pleasure. . . . ."

This child of whom Madame wrote so proudly to her old governess was not destined to survive his third year, but died a few months after the birth of the Duc de Chartres, her second son.

To MADAME VON HARLING.

"April 20th, 1676.

"The terrible blow with which the Almighty has seen fit to overwhelm me so troubled me that I was not able to answer your letter before. You see now how right I was in wishing that my children could be under your care; I always foresaw what would happen to me. They manage children in the strangest way in this country. . . . . . Unfortunately I know nothing about them, never having had any experience, so I am obliged to do what they tell me. The more I think of this the more

wretched I become. I am now quite alone in my grief, for Monsieur started last Thursday with the King to join the army. I fear that all this will injure the child I am awaiting. . . . I do not think that grief can kill—were it so I should certainly have died before now. I cannot describe to you the terrible sufferings I have endured. . . . . ."

The death of the infant Duc de Valois made a permanent impression on Madame's mind as regarded the doctors to whom the royal children were confided.

"May 30th, 1676.

" I wish that I could send you the Duc de Chartres in a letter. I should then feel sure of his life. I fear greatly for him, and would wish him to be three or four years older than he is, and past the dangers of early infancy. They, the doctors, have no idea of the care that children require; they will never listen to anything, and have already dispatched a heap of children into the next world. . . . ."

Shortly after, the Duchess de Chartres, Madame's only daughter and youngest child, was born, and in a letter written ten days after to Madame von Harling, Madame says: " Thank God, the Duc de Chartres is in good health, as is also his little sister, who is as fat as a stuffed goose, and very big for her age. Last Monday they were both christened; they have been given my name and that of Monsieur; thus the rogue is Philippe, and the little girl Charlotte Elizabeth."

We hear that Madame sent for a nurse from Heidelburg for the two children, and stoutly insisted that they should be brought up and physicked German fashion. Keeping herself, during these early years of married life, away from the Court and Court intrigues, Madame led a comparatively happy existence, and her letters during this period are not specially interesting. In 1679 her eldest step-daughter, Marie Louise d'Orléans, married Charles II. of Spain, and was thus added to the already considerable list of people with whom Madame considered it her duty to correspond every week.

In some of Madame's letters to the Raugravine Louise some side-light is thrown on the existence and death of Henrietta of England's unhappy daughter. It is well known that Marie Louise had wished to marry the Dauphin. When she was complaining to the King of having to leave France he is said to have observed, "What could I do more for my own daughter than make her Queen of Spain ? " Whereupon Madame's step-daughter answered, "But you could do more for your niece."

Till the last moment she hoped that the marriage would be broken off. Mme. de Sévigné mentions in more than one letter the Princess's great grief at having to leave France. After leading a most un

happy existence she died in 1689, many thought poisoned by the Comtesse de Soissons, in order that the King of Spain might marry a German Princess.

In the autumn the Court generally migrated to Fontainebleau for a few weeks. From there Madame writes in September, 1677, to the Marquise de Sablé, a lady much esteemed by her; and such were the precautions considered necessary against letters being opened by the messenger that took them that Madame fastened the letter with a black seal across a piece of blue wool. The following proves Madame to have been an accomplished and dignified scribe when writing a ceremonious letter:

" On leaving the chapel this morning I was given your letter, and to prove to you, madame, how greatly I lay store by a faithful and kindly friend, I am going to give up my walk this fine morning in order to answer your letter. The thanks with which you overwhelm me for the poor portrait I sent you, and also all the fine things you are pleased to say to me, causes me to remind you that it makes one feel ashamed to be praised for virtues that one does not really possess however greatly one may long for them. Therefore I beg of you when you gaze at my portrait to remember only this — that the woman before you is your very good friend, and sends you her portrait because she truly loves you.

" CHARLOTTE ELIZABETH."

On the 28th of August, 1680,* the worthy
Elector Karl Ludwig departed this life, and
was much mourned by the good people of
Heidelburg and Manheim to whom he had been
a better father than to his own children.   He
was succeeded by Madame's only brother, who
married, 1681, a Danish princess, and died without posterity in 1685.   A Prince of the House of
Neubourg succeeded him, to Madame's great indignation; she had hoped that the claims of one of
her half-brothers (Louise von Degenfeld's eldest
son) would be recognised.

Madame begins writing about what went on at
Court in the year 1683, just after the death of the
Queen Marie Thérèse; for the event necessarily
raised the wife of Monsieur to the position of first
lady in the kingdom, and obliged her to mix in
Court circles and intrigues.

To the Electress Sophia.

" Saint Cloud, Aug. 1st, 1683.

" I am convinced that you were much surprised
on receiving the sad news of Her Majesty the
Queen's † sudden death.   I own that this event
has grieved me much, for the good Queen was
always my faithful friend through all my troubles,
so you may imagine the pain it has been to me to
see her give up the ghost, after only four days'
illness.   Last Monday night she became feverish,

* Eight years after his daughter's marriage.
† Marie Thérèse, a Spanish princess, married to Louis XIV.

stopped by the Devil, who wished to hear what was going on in France. She replied, 'Alas! I know no news of that kingdom, and never was told any.' Just then up rushes another devil, who cries eagerly, 'Let the Queen pursue her way, I bring somebody who can inform us of everything;' so saying he produces M. Colbert. I tried to learn what *he* said, but nobody has been able to tell me.

"The populace were so incensed with him that they wished to tear his dead body to pieces, and guards had to be placed all the way from his house to the church where they buried him; but they have not been able to prevent a hundred skits and satires being written on the walls of the chapel where he reposes. . . . ."

CHAPTER II.

1686 TO 1692.

"SAINT CLOUD, June 26th, 1686.

"There is an old German proverb which says that when the Devil cannot himself go to a place he sends an old woman; the truth of this is patent to all we members of the royal family, but I will say no more. . . . ."

In this letter Madame first alludes to Mme. de Maintenon, who quickly developed into her pet aversion. Till Louis XIV.'s death they cordially hated one another, and tried in every way to injure one another's credit near the King. Strangely enough neither succeeded; Louis XIV. married Mme. de Maintenon, yet never omitted to show his brother's wife the respect and affection which he considered her due both before and after Monsieur's death.

Madame was perhaps the most aggressive in their quarrels, for she particularly detested the Duc du Maine, Louis XIV. and Mme. de Montespan's son, whom Mme. de Maintenon regarded as her own

child, and persuaded the King to legitimise in a
formal manner. This, as Madame well knew,
might have led to great complications should the
Dauphin die and the King be obliged to declare the
Duc de Chartres his heir.

To the Electress Sophia.

" My son likes copying the manners of grown-up
people, thus the ceremony of the Insignia quite
suited his taste . . . .

" As for ceremonies, my son is exceedingly unlike
me, yet he pretends to like them less than Monsieur, for when asked lately whether he cared for
ceremonies and fine clothes he answered, ' I do not
hate them as does Madame, but then neither do I
share Monsieur's love for them.' "

" Versailles, Aug. 11th, 1686.

" That old wretch, the Maintenon, takes pleasure
in making the King detest all the members of the
royal family with the exception of Monsieur, whom
she praises to him; she manages so that the latter
lives on good terms with his brother, and gives him
all that he asks for. But the moment that Monsieur's
back is turned the old woman fears that she may
be thought to esteem him, so when he is mentioned
she speaks ill of him, saying that he is the most
debauched and false man in the world . . . . .

" All the Ministers have placed themselves under
the heel of this woman,* and try with the lowest

* Mme. de Maintenon.

with fever; this morning the poor little things were bled—I cannot think it a good thing for such little children; the eldest is only five years old.

"I do not think that Charles Louis would find it advantageous to wed a rich French widow and change his religion. No one here cares to see foreigners become Catholic as long as the conversion of the King's subjects is assured. As for taking service in France, I must tell you that the King declared to me that he would not give promotion to any more strangers. Therefore I do not think that Charles Louis can make his way here."

"VERSAILLES, Jan. 26th, 1688.

"It is quite true that diamond crosses are worn, but not from a feeling of devotion. At Court no one is wearing cross-overs, but coiffures are becoming higher every day. The King told us at dinner to-day that a hairdresser, named Allast, dresses the English ladies' hair so high that they can no longer sit upright in their sedan chairs, and so all the ladies now in England are having the top of their chairs altered so as to follow the fashion. . . . ."

"SAINT CLOUD, April 14th, 1688.

"I have been informed secretly that the true reason why the King treats the Marquis d'Effiat and the Chevalier de Lorraine so well is that they have promised him to bring round Monsieur to the idea of soliciting him to allow my children's marrying those of the Montespan. My daughter would thus

have the crippled Duc du Maine, and my son Mdlle. de Blois. In this matter the Maintenon is quite against me, and for the Montespan, for she brought up these wretches, and loves the cripple as much as if she was his own mother. . . . . Now you may imagine what I feel when I think of my daughter being so badly settled in life whilst her sisters * have been so well married. Even were the Duc du Maine † a legitimate Prince of the blood I still would not have him for my son-in-law nor his sister for my daughter-in-law, for she is frightfully ugly and full of other defects. He is as stingy as the devil, and very spiteful. . . . . The worst of it is that I dare not speak frankly to Monsieur, for he has the habit when I tell him anything of going straight to the King and exaggerating greatly whatever I said. He has thus got me into trouble at least a hundred times. I hear that d'Effiat will be given a dukedom, and that the Chevalier will have a large sum of money. . . . . I myself may be exiled—Monsieur speaks of it to me quite seriously. I have never been able to find out whether or not the King is really married to the Maintenon. Many declare that she is his wife, married to him by the Archbishop of Paris in the presence of the King's confessor and the Maintenon's brother; others say that it is impossible, so it is difficult to know the truth. But it is

* The daughters of Henrietta of England.
† The son of Louis XIV. and Mme. de Montespan.

certain that the King never cared for any of his former mistresses with the same intensity that he does for this woman. . . . ."

There is now no doubt that Louis XIV. was married to Mme. de Maintenon by Monseigneur Harlai, Archbishop of Paris, in 1685, in the presence of Père la Chaise and the Marquis de Montchevruil, not the brother, but an old friend of both Scarron and his widow.

Mme. de Maintenon was extremely anxious that she should be acknowledged Queen Consort before the King's death, but this he always refused to do, acting, it is said, by Fénélon's advice, but Madame de *Maintenant,* as her old friend Ninon de l'Enclos nicknamed her, had unbounded influence. The Pope frequently wrote to her, and she had spies and correspondents in every European Court, and knew all that was going on far better than the King's Ministers. Madame and she had rival 'inquiry offices,' so between the two the French Court was kept well supplied with news.

To the Electress Sophia.
" Saint Cloud, Aug. 2nd, 1688.

" The grande Mademoiselle has gone to Eu, where she is to spend two months. I do not know what the King can have said to her, but she looks far from pleased. When I bade her good-bye last Saturday she wished to tell me, but I pretended not to understand what she was alluding to. One

cannot trust this worthy Mademoiselle in the least. To-day she tries to pleasure you; to-morrow she seeks to do you an injury. She repeats everything said to her with amplifications; for these reasons I thought it most prudent to remain silent."

" Saint Cloud, Sept. 26th, 1688.

" In the meanwhile our Dauphin has become a warrior. As I have already told you he started yesterday to besiege and take possession of Phillipsbourg. He told me that after accomplishing that he would take Manheim and Frankanthal, and generally speaking defend my interests, but I answered, 'If you take my advice you will remain at home, for I own to you that I feel grieved, not pleased, at the thought that my name will be used to ruin my poor country.' * On this we parted."

To Madame's great anger France set up a claim to the Palatinate on her behalf, Louvois persuading the King and the royal family that with a few vigorous measures the Palatinate would be abandoned by the Neubourgs and annexed to France as part of Madame's dowry. This led to the devastation of the states, to which Madame so often and so bitterly alludes during the next ten years. Obliged by Louis XIV's policy to represent herself as desirous to recover her rights over her father's and brother's succession, in many documents which she was never even shown, Madame

* The Palatinate.

protested in all her private letters against France's action in the matter, and made every one at court thoroughly aware of her grief and disapproval of what the King was doing on her behalf.

To the Electress Sophia.

"Fontainebleau, Nov. 19th, 1688.

"I deferred writing to you till I received your honoured letter of the 18th-28th October, then I understood how you shared my grief for our loss. Although I weep less than at first, I feel a great interior sadness and melancholy. I see that it will be a long time before I shall console myself for the loss of that good Charles Louis.* My troubles are increased by hearing all those round me discuss incessantly the preparations that are being made to burn and bombard the good town of Manheim, which my father, the late Elector, built with so much care. It makes my heart bleed, yet they are angry at my grief. . . . . . Although Monsieur asked the King to allow homage to be rendered him, his petition was refused. Now the King is sole master in the Palatinate. But I am far from thinking that he will give anything to the Margrave's children, for the virtue of charity is rarely practised here.

"During the ten days that I lay ill in Paris, the King never sent for news of me. I wrote to him; he has not yet answered. When I returned here, I

* Madame's half-brother, killed at the siege of Négrepont.

I think of all that has been destroyed, that every
night I think myself at Heidelburg or Manheim,
in the middle of the desolation. I wake up with a
start and do not go to sleep again for two hours. I
think of it all as I once knew it, and as it is now;
also of the change in my own life, and then I cannot prevent myself weeping. What is also painful
is that the King actually waited before reducing
them to where they are now, for my intreaties in
favour of Heidelburg and Manheim. . . . . . I felt
sure that you would be much grieved at the death
of our good Queen of Spain ;* so to speak, I cannot
yet digest it. Although following the example of
all her Majesty's near and high relatives, I have
resumed going to all the Court festivities, I come
back from them as sad as I went· · · · · ·"

"SAINT CLOUD, May 20th, 1689.

"I see that Monsieur is thinking of appointing
the Marquis d'Effiat governor to my son. He is
my worst enemy, and will set my son against me
as he has already done my husband. · · · · ·

"Our Raugraves† are very unfortunate in thus
losing all their rights. If I had any money I would
send them some with all my heart, but you cannot
think how poor I am myself. I have only a hundred
pistoles a month, and I can never give less than
a pistole for anything ; at the end of eight days all

* Madame's step-daughter, Marie Louise d'Orléans.
† Madame's half-brothers.

is spent—everything has passed in fruit, flowers, and
stamps. When the King gives me anything I have
to pay up old debts, and he only gives presents
for the new year. Monsieur has never given me a
groat. If I wish to buy the least little thing I have
to borrow; this renders it impossible for me to give
gifts. Even if I sent for Charles Maurice * and
made an *abbé* of him he would never obtain any
benefices. They are rare just now. Quite lately
the Prince de Talmont, son of the Princesse de
Tarente, had to resign orders and become a soldier
because they allowed him to starve."

"SAINT CLOUD, June 5th, 1689.

"Our Dauphiness becomes feebler every day.
At first the doctors, to please certain old women
whom I refrain from naming, for you will guess
to whom I refer, declared that the Dauphine was
hypochondriacal, and that her illness only existed
in her own imagination ; they have allowed the
disease to increase to such a degree that I fear
nothing will save her. Now that she has to lie
abed they are obliged to own that she is really
ill, but they are extremely ignorant. . . . ."

"VERSAILLES, June 30th, 1689.

"M. de Behenac is not wrong in thinking that
the good Queen of Spain was poisoned. The fact
was plain when they opened her ; immediately
after death she became purple, which is, they say,

* One of Madame's half-brothers.

D 2

a great proof of poison. What again makes some believe that she was poisoned by oysters, is, that one of her maids, wishing also to swallow one, was hurriedly prevented from doing so by some grandee, who snatched it from her, saying that she would fall ill if she partook of it.

"I hear that one of the Princesses Palatine * is going to be the new Queen of Spain. They have made a fine story of it here, saying that she is in love with Prince Louis of Baden, and that it is for this reason that she is reluctant to become Queen of Spain."

"VERSAILLES, July 21st, 1689.

"Last year the Dauphiness called me into her boudoir, and informed me with tears in her eyes that everyone was talking of the love my cousin, de la Tremouille, entertained for her, and that all blamed her much for allowing it. She begged me to tell my cousin to abstain from coming so frequently into her presence, and to leave off certain of his ways. . . . . I told her that it would be better if she would despise that sort of talk, but she still asked me to do as she wished. I did so, and also scolded him well, but he answered that he was unhappy, not guilty, and that as soon as he had finished his service he would ask leave to absent himself to go to his mother † in Ger-

* One of the Princesses belonging to the Neuburg branch.
† The Princesse de Tarente, née Princess of Hesse.

many; or, if the Dauphiness judged it necessary, he would sell his commission and live on his property. I told her all this; she replied that all she asked was that he should only come into her apartments with the King, have less free manners, and be careful as to his expression when looking at her. I heard nothing more for some time, but a fortnight since he came to me saying that the Duchesse d'Arpajon, lady-in-waiting to the Dauphiness, had caused him to be fetched, and had ordered him from her mistress never to approach her again. . . . . You cannot imagine how much the Dauphiness has been blamed in this matter."

"SAINT CLOUD, Oct. 30th, 1689.

"I was told yesterday a thing that touched me so deeply that I could not help shedding tears. The poor inhabitants of Manheim have retired into their cellars, living there entirely, even holding their market there daily as though the town was still in its old state. When a Frenchman visits Heidelburg the poor people rush at him and ask for news of me, speaking eagerly of my father and brother. . . . ."

"VERSAILLES, Feb. 8th, 1690.

"The poor Dauphiness is again very ill. She is now under the care of a Capuchin monk, who goes by the name of Frère Ange. It is said that he cured the Duke of Bavaria and his wife of very dangerous diseases. Would to God that he succeeds equally well in this case, but up to the present time there is no sign of it. They are killing her with worry. Everything was once done to reduce me to a like state; but I am a harder nut to crack than the Dauphiness, and before they have come to the end of me the old women will break some of their teeth."

"VERSAILLES, June 12th, 1690.

"It was quite impossible for me to reply to your second letter at Saint Cloud. I wept so bitterly at the funeral* of the poor Dauphiness that for two days I could see to do nothing. Not only was I grieved at the loss of the Dauphiness, whom I was very fond of, but the sight of our arms† everywhere—on the coffin, on the hangings of the church, etc.—recalled to me so vividly the death of His Highness, my father, that of my mother, and of my brother, that I feared I should burst with emotion.

"The Wednesday after this terrible ceremony we went to Marly, and stayed there till Saturday. My grief ought to have been lightened, for everything went on as usual—the apartments full of gamblers, hunting every afternoon, and music in the evening; yet all this only increased my melancholy."

* This ceremony lasted six hours.
† The Palatinate and Bavarian royal families both possessed the same arms. The Dauphiness was a Bavarian Princess.

"VERSAILLES, July 30th, 1690.

"When the King of England * had got into his coach to go back to Saint Germains, he found, when only a few yards from the gates of the chateau, one of his servants, who announced to him that it was reported all through Ireland that Marshal Schomberg had been badly wounded, and the young Prince of Orange had died from the effect of his wounds. We have since learnt that what was said about the poor Marshal was quite true, but that the Prince was only slightly wounded. You can form no idea of the joy provoked by the news of his death; guards had to be sent to calm the tumult, but they found themselves powerless; it lasted about forty-eight hours, during which the populace did nothing but eat and drink. The Cordeliers † did light a great bonfire in front of their convent, and danced singing round it. It is strange that the King with all his power could not hinder this. · · · ·

"The King of England is not quick in repartee—sometimes he would be wiser if he kept silence. All the same, I must tell you of a conversation that he held with my gentleman-in-waiting· · · · ·

"'Sire,' said M. de la Rougère, 'what became of the French who were with your Majesty?' 'I know nothing of them,' replied the King. 'How so?' said La Rougère, 'Your Majesty knows nothing of them? were they not with you?' 'Pardon me,' answered the King, 'but I am going

* James II.   † A monastic order.

special protection. This was enough to incense
Madame against them, but as time went on her
feelings greatly altered, and she finished by having
a hearty affection for *le bon roy* and his sensible,
courageous wife.

Encouraged by Louis XIV., James II. made a
futile attempt to recover his lost throne, but Fate
proved unkind, and James left Ireland a sadder
and a wiser man, to live and die in the home
offered to him by the King of France.

TO THE ELECTRESS SOPHIA.

"SAINT CLOUD, Aug. 20th, 1690.

"Herewith I send you all the ditties that are
being sung; they are not exactly complimentary
to our worthy King of England, and you will see
on reading them that although the King is beloved
and the Prince of Orange hated, yet the people
here hold the latter in most respect. Last Thursday we received a visit from the poor King and
Queen; she was serious, he very gay. I over-
heard a dialogue which greatly diverted me. Monsieur, as usual, was talking of his jewels and furniture, and ended by saying to the King: 'And
your Majesty who has so much money, have you
built some fine palace?' 'Money!' observed the
Queen, 'he never had any. I never saw him with
a halfpenny.' The King answered, 'I once had
some, but I did not purchase gems and furniture,
neither did I build palaces, all mine went in

making fine ships, cannons and muskets.' ' Yes,' said the Queen, ' and much good it did you. Everything has gone ill with us.' Thus ended the conversation. If the prophecy of the late King of England comes true, King James will not even make a good saint. Mme. de Portsmouth, whom we had here a short time since, told me that the late King used to say, ' You see my brother? When he becomes King he will surely lose his kingdom through religious zeal, and his soul through ugly queans, for he has too bad taste to choose fine ones.' This prophecy is already coming true; his kingdom is lost, and I heard that it is said in Dublin that he brought there two ugly things whom he never left. . . . .

"The more one sees of this King, and the more one hears about the Prince of Orange, the more one feels bound to excuse the latter and find him worthy of esteem. No doubt you are now saying to yourself that one always comes back to one's first love,* but it is certain that an intelligence such as his pleases me more than a handsome face. . . . ."

Madame was very fond of William III. So much so that after the death of Queen Mary she hoped that he would marry her daughter the young Duchess de Chartres, and so prevent the latter

* William of Orange was Madame's cousin ; she became acquainted with him in her youth, when she spent some time in Holland during the year 1661.

to do like that Englishman named Fildin (Fielding). It happened in this wise some years ago. Wendt asked him once at Fontainebleau, 'Are you a Huguenot, monsieur?' 'No,' said he. 'So you are Catholic,' observed Wendt. 'Even less,' replied the Englishman. 'Ah!' said Wendt again, 'then you are a Lutheran.' 'Not at all,' replied Fildin. 'What are you then?' says Wendt. 'I will inform you,' replied the Englishman. 'I have a little religion apart for myself.' Good King James would also have been wiser had he thus acted instead of losing three kingdoms * through bigotry . . . . ."

" Fontainebleau, Oct. 20th, 1690.

"Since I have learnt to know the good King well I have become very fond of him. He is the best man in the world, and I pity him with all my heart, for sometimes he sighs in a heartrending fashion. He took me aside and put me through a regular examination as to whether it was true that his daughter, the Princess of Orange, had taken his misfortune so much to heart that she had refused to dance on the occasion of the Electress of Brandeburg's visit to the Hague. . . . ."

" Versailles, Dec. 5th, 1690.

"I am somewhat more in favour this year than last. I do not know to whom I owe this happiness,

---

* England, Scotland, and Ireland.

suspected of having instilled poison into a silver vessel from which M. de Louvois drank that afternoon. We shall soon know the truth about it. . . . As he was destined to die I could wish that he could have done so three years ago; the poor Palatine States would have benefited."

"SAINT CLOUD, Aug. 23rd, 1691.

"I have already informed you of the death of M. de Louvois. If it is true that he died from poison, I do not believe that it is from the act of his sons, bad as they may be. I am more inclined to think that it is the work of some doctor who wished to please a certain old woman,* whom M. de Louvois greatly offended, and of whom he spoke with great freedom to the King on his way to Mons. The King looks far from being displeased by this death; I have seldom seen him so merry as now. . . ."

"FONTAINEBLEAU, Sept. 28th, 1691.

"M. de Louvois is so forgotten that no one now cares whether he was poisoned or not. His son, M. de Barbezieux, is going to be married soon, and to a lady that once was to be married to his eldest brother, M. de Courtenveau. The lady, Mdlle. d'Uzes, preferred the youngest, in which matter she showed judgment, for the elder one is stupid and very ugly, whilst Barbezieux is

* Allusion to Madame de Maintenon.

very clever and amiable. They are equally well off. Although the eldest one had seemed much in love he immediately resigned himself to his brother's desire, but I fancy that the latter had better abstain from eating with him, for he poisoned his governor in Rome. Our great man * is incapable of such things. I know that certain people have offered to assassinate the Prince of Orange for him, but he never consented; but I feel sure that many are animated by this indiscreet zeal. All the same the Prince of Orange must have a great deal of moral courage to be so little afraid of death; no one can deny that he is a worthy man."

Madame had three half-sisters, to whom she was greatly attached, and with whom she corresponded constantly. After the Elector Karl Ludwig's death his daughters were obliged to leave Heidelburg. The Electress Sophia, who had always accepted Louise von Degenfeld as a sister-in-law, took them in, and the Raugravines Caroline, Louise, and Amelia followed their aunt from Hanover to England, where the eldest, Caroline, married the son of Marshal Schomberg. To this lady Madame wrote but rarely; with the two others, who returned to Germany shortly after their sister's marriage, she kept up an active correspondence, which increased greatly after the Electress Sophia's death. But long before that event took place Madame wrote every week to the

* Louis XIV.

CHAPTER III.

1692 TO 1696.

Mme. de Maintenon persuaded the King to give Mdlle. de Blois* in marriage to the Duc de Chartres, Monsieur's son, representing to him that he would thus secure a hold over his somewhat flighty nephew. Although Madame must have been well aware of this plot against her most cherished ideas and feelings she said but little about it in her letters. When Monsieur cautiously proposed the thing to her on behalf of the King, she burst into tears and declared that nothing would induce her to give her consent to her son's thus disgracing himself by marrying the King's illegitimate daughter, but on Louis XIV. sending for her she gave in. Saint Simon gives a strange picture of the Duc de Chartres coming up to his mother in the great gallery at Versailles and being received with a smart box on the ear before the whole Court, assembled together to have the marriage officially announced.

* Daughter of Mme. de Montespan.

E

To the Electress Sophia.
"Versailles, Feb. 21st, 1692.

" You were ill-informed by those who told you
that I had behaved like a child on the occasion of
my son's marriage. I am no longer of an age to
indulge in childish conduct. . . . . . As for my
daughter-in-law I shall not be much troubled by
her, as we shall not be so often together as to get
tired of one another. She is in the King's set,
which is a *sanctum sanctorum*, where simple mortals
such as myself do not enter. As for the advan-
tages that will accrue to my son, I only hope that
they will be as brilliant as you have been told
they will be; but as everything consists as yet
in promises and hopes, I am not charmed with
the whole affair; I own that I have never been
able to understand how it is that Monsieur, who
gets on so admirably with his brother, was not
able to persuade the King to give his nephew
enough to uphold his rank without forcing him
to make such an unequal marriage- . . . ."

" Paris, March 5th, 1692.

" Thank God for all his mercies ! M. du Maine's
marriage is a settled thing, so one of my troubles
is thus lifted from me. I fancy that they have
informed the King's old wretch* what was being
said in Paris, and that it frightened her. The
people were saying that although it was a disgrace

* Allusion to Mme. de Maintenon.

for the King to arrange a marriage between one of
his bastards and a Prince of the blood belonging to
his family, yet, as the husband confers rank on the
woman he weds, they would allow that marriage
to take place, though much against their feelings ;
but that if the old woman took it into her head to
give my daughter to M. du Maine, they would
strangle him before the wedding, and that the old
woman whom they still style his governess should
not be sure of her life. Whilst all this was being
said, the rumour arose of the other marriage with
the Prince's daughter, which pleases everybody in
Paris. I am grateful to the worthy Parisians for
their having thus felt an interest in me.

" I am going to tell you what I have learnt of
the sayings of Mme. Cornuel. I do not know if
you ever heard of this lady. She is more than
eighty years old, but is as lively as though she
was only twenty-five. She it is who said once
of our King of England, after having seen His
Majesty, ' Let our King do what he will, and
behave well to the King of England, he will never
make anything better of him than poor man's
sauce.' Lately she came to Court and saw Mme.
de Maintenon and M. de Barbezieux. ' I saw,' said
she, ' the most singular thing in the world when
at Court—Love in the grave and the Ministry in the
cradle.' "

" Versailles, April 12th, 1692.
" It is to be hoped that after all our waiting
E 2

we shall finally be able to catch the Duc de Bour-gogne; * he would not be a bad morsel. You are too good to look thas at the monkey-cat-bear visage of my daughter, but her figure is far from being a bad one. . . . ."

"SAINT CLOUD, May 1st, 1692.

"Time alone will show us what will be the result of this descent upon England, but it is difficult to suppose that the Prince of Orange will allow the three kingdoms to be taken from him, as easily as he contrived to take them from his father-in-law. . . . ."

"PARIS, May 15th, 1692.

"I hear that the King of England can only have embarked last Sunday. Tourville has an order, signed by the King's own hand, to attack the enemy as soon as they find them. So we shall soon receive the news of a naval battle. . . . ."

"SAINT CLOUD, May 22nd, 1692.

"Although these good people are my neigh-bours, I cannot love them as myself, and when I examine my conscience I can only see one thing —which is that I care for those that love me or at least who do not hate me. In this matter I find it most difficult to follow the Holy Scriptures. . . . ."

"PARIS, June 8th, 1692.

"The King's old monster has enjoyed this great power for a long time. She is not such a fool as

* For her daughter.

to get herself acknowledged Queen; she knows he good man's temper too well. If she did such t thing she would soon fall into disgrace and be utterly lost.

"The Venetian Ambassador has spread about in the King's army that my uncle * had given a million (of francs) to the Emperor to be made Prince Elector. It seems to me that my uncle might have made a better bargain.

"King William and our people are now close upon one another. Would to God that there be no battle! The great man † is in bed; he is il with an attack of gout. I think that the nava battle will not prove a soothing remedy for hi ills. . . . ."

"SAINT CLOUD, June 12th, 1692.

"The news of a great battle will soon be here My heart beats when I think of it; to tell the truth, a river flows between our people and the enemy, but I hear that the Prince of Orange i making bridges. I am in great trouble on accoun of my boy."

"SAINT CLOUD, June 19th, 1692.

"To tell the truth, and nothing but the truth our good King James is an honest and worthy man but one of the silliest that I have ever seen; t child of seven years old would not make such piti ful mistakes—piety renders him idiotic. . . . .

* The Duke of Hanover.   † Louis XIV.

"I would lay my head that our King neither approved nor ordered the assassination,* he is incapable of such a thing. But what makes me think that it is the old woman's doing is that I have heard that she told the King that she had learnt from a sure source, that the Prince of Orange had sent someone to Philippeville to poison the fountains . . . . You see by this what she is capable of, for I am sure that the Prince thought as little of poisoning the fountains as I do of going to hang myself. . . . ."

"SAINT CLOUD, Aug. 9th, 1692.

"I must tell you about the fright I had last Monday, which thank God soon became changed into joy. I was already undressed and just getting into bed at midnight, when I suddenly heard Mon' voice in my antechamber. Knowing that he already gone to bed, I got up and ran to meet him to see what was the matter. In his hand he held an open letter, and he said to me, 'Do not be frightened, your son has been wounded, but only slightly; there has been a great battle in Flanders; the King's infantry defeated that of the Prince of Orange; all this is only just known; the King tells me that no further details have yet arrived.' I leave you to imagine the anguish given me by this news. I stayed on my balcony till three o'clock in the morning to see if any messenger came from

* Grandval's plot. See Macaulay's *William III.* vol. 3, chap. i.

my son; one arrived about every half-hour; once was brought the news of the Marquis de Bellefond's death; again the announcement that M. de Turenne was wounded to death; his mother and his mother-in-law, Mme. de Ventadour, who loves him like a son, are here; they are just above my chamber and I can hear their cries. . . .

"At last, the next day after lunch, a gentleman arrived who had once been sub-governor to my son—he is called La Bertière. He told us that my son had been shot twice, once his cloak had been shattered, but he not touched, thank God! the other ball penetrated into his left arm, but he got it out himself. His arm bound up and the wound attended to, he returned to the scene of action and remained there till all was over. . . . At first our people gave way, the English and Dutch were getting over the hedges and ditches, they had already taken three cannons, when M. de Luxembourg arrived with the guards, the Prince de Conti, the Duke, and my son. They rallied the hussars and led them forward themselves towards the enemy. This inspired the soldiers with fresh courage, so much so that they broke down everything and threw the enemy so far back that they not only regained their own cannons but took seven from the others . . . ."

"SAINT CLOUD, Sept. 18th, 1692.

"*Apropos* of letters opened at the poste, allow me to tell you the story of a thing which happened several years ago. The Grande Mademoiselle receives several letters from her business people, and perceives clearly that they have been opened. When answering them she adds, 'As M. de Louvois is very clever, and as he will see this letter before it reaches you, I beg of him, when opening it, to add a little advice on my affairs, which will certainly be the better for it;' since then they have not opened her letters."

"VERSAILLES, Jan. 1st, 1693.

"There is more stealing than ever going on in Paris. The other day some thieves saw a coach in which sat two ladies, who had diamond ornaments stuck into their headdresses. They began to call out, 'Stop, stop! the wheel of your coach is broken, you will be upset.' The coachman stops, wishing to see what has happened; the ladies also, they put their heads out of the window, the robbers seize the headdresses, diamonds and all, and make off. . . . ."

"MARLY, April 9th, 1693.

"Our worthy Grande Mademoiselle has at last come to the end of her troubles. She died Sunday at six o'clock in the evening, and Monday the First President opened her will. Monsieur is universal legatee. She leaves the Dauphin her fine house at Choisy, founds several hospitals, and leaves something to all her servants. This is what is embodied in her will. Yesterday we rendered her the last honours, giving her holy water, in

long cloaks and hoods. She died from the ignorance of her doctors; they did not know from what she was suffering, and stuffed her so with emetics that the inflammation set in which carried her off.

"To make people think that he was really married to her, Lauzun asked a lady in marriage immediately after her death, although he knew the former was engaged, and that the King had already signed the contract. The day after the will was opened, that is to say Tuesday, he showed himself before the King and royal family in a long cloak. After having stayed three-quarters of an hour with Monsieur, he left the chamber, returning a moment afterwards with a large packet, sealed six times with Mademoiselle's own seal. This he presented to Monsieur, saying, '*Apropos*, I forgot to give you this paper, which Mademoiselle gave six years ago to Madame de Noguet to keep for her' (she is Lauzun's sister). Monsieur replied that he could not open the packet, that it must be sent to the First President. This packet greatly troubled the Dauphin and Monsieur, for if it had been another will made six years ago they would have inherited nothing, as the one opened just after Mademoiselle's death was dated eight years ago, in 1685. At midnight Monsieur was told that the packet had been opened, and had contained a will dated 1670. Lauzun, who must have known this, probably wished to amuse himself ; this shows him to be wicked—an ungrateful animal."

"COLOMBES, Aug. 22nd, 1693.

"My son led the cavalry he commands five different times at the enemy, and during two hours he stood under fire . . . . If my son did not serve in a campaign every year he would be despised and lose all consideration."

"PARIS, 23 Dec., 1694.

"We nearly lost our theatre lately. The Sorbonne, to please the King, tried to forbid it, but the Archbishop of Paris and Father La Chaise must have told them that it would be too dangerous to put an end to innocent amusements, as it would lead to the young falling into real vices. . . . I shall continue to go to the theatre till they put an end to it. A fortnight ago there was a sermon against theatres, saying that play-acting revived evil passions. The King turned to me and said, 'He is not preaching at me who no longer go to the theatre, but at you others who go and approve.' 'Although I am fond of comedies,' I answered, 'and go there frequently, M. d'Agen is not thinking of me, for he only speaks of those who go there to revive their passions, which I do not do. The theatre simply amuses me, there is no harm in that.' The King did not say a word more. . . ."

"VERSAILLES, Jan. 16th, 1695.

"The theatre is always so full in Paris that the

spectators are mixed up with the actors, which is very disagreeable. Then again nothing can be more dull than our evenings in Paris ; Monsieur plays at lansquenet at a large table ; but I am not allowed to approach or show myself, for Monsieur thinks that I bring him ill-luck, yet he obliges me to stay in the apartment, so all the old women who do not play have to be entertained by me. This goes on from seven to ten, and makes me yawn frightfully. Every two days I have to go after dinner to Port-Royal, so as not to break one of my oldest customs, but I no longer go with the same pleasure as before."

"VERSAILLES, Feb. 3rd, 1695.

"The cold is so intense that one hardly knows what to do. Yesterday, during high mass, I thought that my feet were becoming frozen, for when with the King no one is allowed foot-warmers. I had a very funny conversation with our King. He was scolding me for wearing a scarf. 'No one has ever been in the procession with a scarf,' said he. 'Perhaps so,' replied I ; 'but we have never had such cold weather before.' 'Before this time you never wore one,' said the King. 'Before this time I was younger and more able to bear the cold,' I observed. 'There were many older than you are who did not wear any scarves,' said he. 'In that case,' I replied, 'those old women preferred to be frozen to putting on an ugly thing, and I prefer to be badly dressed than that my chest should freeze, for I do not go in for vanities.' To this he answered naught."

Madame had many similar passages-at-arms with the King. His extreme piety greatly troubled her, for as she grew older she found great pleasure in going to the play, one of the things Louis XIV. took to disliking in his old age, and she feared lest he might prevail on the Archbishop of Paris to forbid the playhouses as scandalous and frivolous. As the following will prove, Madame could not be accused of vanity by her contemporaries.

To the Raugravine Louise.

"Versailles, March 5th, 1695.

"I do not understand why people require so many different costumes; my only habiliments consist of my grand State robe, and my riding-habit when I hunt on horseback; nothing else. I never in my whole life wore a dressing-gown or mantle, and in my wardrobe there is but one bed-gown in which I get in and out of bed.

"I felt sure that Caroline * would take much to heart Queen Mary's † death. All those who knew her praised her exceedingly. King James of England, whom we have here, did not wish us to go into mourning for his daughter; indeed, he begged us not to do so. This greatly surprised me, for I think that one cannot forget one's own children

---

* Madame's half-sister, married to Marshal Schomberg.
† Mary, daughter of James II., married to William of Orange.

however badly they have behaved; surely blood is thicker than water. After the description given me of Prince William I should not have thought him so attached to his wife; I grieve for him with all my heart. If I had been allowed to I should have written to Caroline charging her with my compliments and condolences. It is so bitterly cold that the wine as well as water freezes in the glasses at the King's table."

To the Electress Sophia.

"Marly, March 16th, 1695.

" 6 o'clock in the evening.

"The most important thing is that King William's health is re-established; his grief will pass away in the course of time. Just now the King allows me to sleep all through the sermon . . . . ."

" Choisy, April 7th, 1695.

"The *Amadis* * greatly amused me. This is the reason why I remember it all so well, but I had not the patience to read the whole twenty-four volumes as did my uncle. . . . . I do not believe that the Abbé de Locume will soon attain his wish of uniting together all the sects of the Christian religion, for where material interests are at stake people do not easily give way. I do not think that M. de Meaux* wishes it; if everyone was of the same faith, bishops and priests would have nothing left to say. . . . ."

---

* A much-read romance.   † Bossuet.

"Paris, May 1st, 1695.

"I think that since piety has become the fashion at Court, dramatic authors imagine that their pieces would be more welcome if they added in a little devotion. At first their plan succeeded, but now no one can bear their comedies. When the actors announced that they were going to give another play of this sort, the pit called out, ' We don't want any more of that sort! ' ' Why so?' replied the others, 'it has been much applauded.' The pit replied, ' This play * was not hissed because it was acted during Lent, and we were all occupied in hissing the Abbé Boileau's sermon at Versailles.' This was an amusing answer."

To the Raugravine Louise.
"Paris, May 14th, 1695.

"Dancing is no longer the fashion. Here as soon as a few find themselves together they begin to play at lansquenet; it is the game most in vogue; young men no longer care to dance. As for me I do neither the one nor the other, being much too old for dancing, having indeed given it up on our father's death. I never play for two very good reasons: firstly, that I have no money; secondly, that I do not care for gambling. Enormous sums are played for here, the players being as those possessed; one yells, another strikes the table so hard with his fist that the whole room shakes, a third swears in such a manner as to cause one's hair to

* *Judith*, a tragedy by the Abbé Boyer.

stand on end—all seem not themselves, and are fearful to witness.

"In Paris one does not enjoy very fine weather, yet I go out in my coach when I can; twice I rode at a stag-hunt; perhaps you will say that I am too old to go a-hunting, and I quite agree, still I prefer to be ridiculous to being ill, and there is nothing better for my pains than violent exercise and riding, so I bravely continue to hunt."

"Fontainebleau, Oct. 8th, 1695.

"I am very grateful to you for rejoicing with me on my son's arrival. He was ill some little time, but since he is here he has got better, through playing and hunting, and is quite well now, thank God.

"Marshal de Boufflers has certainly been celebrated in song here. Here are some verses composed in his honour—they are sung on the tune of *Joconde* :

> ' Quoy Boufflier duo (?) on a grand tord,
>   C'est insulter la France.
> Guillaume l'aurait fait milord
>   C'est sa vray récompense, etc.'

"You see by this that everything is here put into verse.

"You speak of your face, which you style old-fashioned: you forget that I am ten years older than you are. It is not my place to speak of others' faces—I neither like nor hate people on

To the Electress Sophia.

"Fontainebleau, Oct. 22nd, 1695.

"The tone has quite changed about King William;* one hears everywhere, 'He is a great King, and worthy of his position. His is a master mind,' and similar things. You are indeed right when you say that only those in luck ever get the world's praise—this is why King William is so much thought of. Everything here is settled by fashion, they speak only too freely of both friends and foes. Royal blood does not shield one—indeed lampoons are generally written about crowned heads. . . . . ."

To the Raugravine Louise.

"Marly, Dec. 1st, 1695.

"Herr Fabricius writes me that he intends coming to Saint Cloud when peace is declared. I have not time to-day to answer his epistle; pray thank him for me, and say that I shall be delighted to see him at Saint Cloud. Between ourselves, if he comes here he must never call me your Highness; this title is good for the Princes of the blood; we and our children are styled 'Royal Highness;' only the children of France have right to this title. . . . ."

"Versailles, Dec. 11th, 1695.

"I feel greatly pleased on being told that I am said to have a German heart, and that I love my country. I shall try with God's help to merit this

* William III. of England.

F

account till the day of my death. My heart is still German, for I cannot console myself for what has happened in the poor Palatinate; when I think of it I am sad the whole day.

"Nothing can be more wretched than the fate destined to Queens in Spain. I know this from the late Queen, who recounted to me the life she led day by day. In Portugal it is even worse, and shows the truth of that saying, 'All that glitters is not gold.'"

CHAPTER IV.

1696 to 1698.

"Versailles, Jan. 1st, 1696.

"The messenger Lasalle would indeed have given me pleasure by bringing your portraits. I will try and find out which way the rogue came. I will send you mine (portrait) in my hunting-habit, because this likeness is, or rather was, the best of me ever done; for since I had the small pox I have not cared to be painted—just now I am uglier than ever."

To the Electress Sophia.
"Versailles, Feb. 5th, 1696.

"During the last two days that I spent in Paris two different persons came and asked me whether I was aware of what was being said about me; the Chevalier de Bouillon seems to have boasted publicly, both at the theatre and at the opera, that I was greatly in love with him, and this he said in such insolent terms that no one dared to repeat them to me. I answered that anything said by the Chevalier de Bouillon could injure nobody, as owing

F 2

to his being a drunkard and a liar his word is
never taken, but that if he continued these amiable discourses about me I should cover him with
such ridicule as should last him his lifetime. After
this I neither saw nor thought of the Chevalier de
Bouillon, till last Monday, going into our theatre
here, I perceived some young men laughing at me,
and pointing to the Chevalier. This aroused my
anger. We were talking of the word 'to accost,'
so I said aloud, 'There is a fellow up there that I
shall soon accost.' 'Who?' asked the Dauphin.
'The Chevalier de Bouillon,' I replied; 'I hear
from all sides that he boasts of my affection for
him: as this is news to me I mean to ask him
which are the great and good qualities that have so
touched me; and if he continues his amiabilities
I shall be forced to ask the King to send far away
the torch which is reducing my heart to ashes,' I
ended laughing.

" The Dauphin immediately told my son to command the Chevalier never to find himself in my
presence again. That same evening his father,
M. de Bouillon, came to me and said how grieved
he was to think of his son being falsely accused
of insulting me. He asked me to inform him of
the people who had told me: if men, his son
should fight them; if women, he would cut off their
noses. I began to laugh and replied, 'The King
has forbidden all forms of duelling, but your son
would have plenty to do for some time to come

think that war is the cause, for it gives them the
tone and manners of common soldiers. . . . ."

To the Electress Sophia.

"Marly, March 1st, 1696.

"We are soon going to have a weary time here,
for a Jubilee is due. This is ill-named, as nothing
can be more wearisome. One must be perpetually
stuck in church, eat fish, always fast, and communicate. Again, all the time the thing continues,
no amusements, operas, or plays are allowed. King
James will celebrate his Jubilee on sea, for he
went off yesterday to Calais, where he will embark
with an army for England. *Sal den tied lerm**
what will come of it. . . . ."

To the Raugravine Louise.

"Versailles, March 25th, 1696.

"I was already too old when I came to France
to change my character. This is not surprising,
for the base of it was laid before I arrived. But I
should be indeed inexcusable were I deceitful and
double-faced, and if I did not love those for whom
I ought to feel affection. You are right in saying
that I write what I feel to be the truth. . . . ."

To the Electress Sophia.

"Versailles, April 1st, 1696.

"The French cannot forego the pleasure of
making fun of others. They must laugh at all
they hear. Now that they see that King James

* "Time must show us." (Dutch.)

one for Monsieur and had not been paid, he imagined that I should not pay either, and so avoided obeying me. . . . ."

"VERSAILLES, May 13th, 1696.

" I have found another painter now, and hope to be able to send you and Caroline the three portraits in time. . . . .

" It seems that King William is not at all cruel, for he himself took care to give his father-in-law time to escape with his family. I think that he does not wish harm to come to the Duke of Berwick on account of the latter's extraordinary likeness to his wife (Queen Mary). Our Queen of England * here has a portrait of her late daughter-in-law; when she showed it me I thought that it was the Duke of Berwick in petticoats. Of course they are such near relations that this likeness is not surprising. Now it is evident here that King William is a man of heart, and I was in the right when I said so."

To THE ELECTRESS SOPHIA.

"MARLY, May 16th, 1696.

" One cannot image how silly the great man is where religion is concerned—he is so in nothing else. It is because he has never read anything treating of religion, or the Bible, so he believes anything told him on these matters. Then, when he had a mistress who was not pious, he gave up piety

* Mary of Modena.

too, but since he has fallen in love with a woman who talks of nothing but penance, he believes all that she says, to such a point that when the lady and the confessor disagree he puts more faith in her than in the other."

"SAINT CLOUD, May 20th, 1696.

" I must own that when I hear the great man praised in a sermon for his persecution of the reformed, I am always impatient; I cannot hear bad actions being praised."

"SAINT CLOUD, May 23rd, 1696.

" I do not like kings thinking that they please the Lord much by prayer. It is not for that that He has placed them on thrones, but to do good—administer justice fairly and rightly. In these actions ought we to see kings' devotions. Also they ought to see that priests keep to their prayers, and not meddle with anything else. When a king says his morning and evening prayers, he has done all he need; again, he ought to make his subjects as happy as he can. . . ."

"SAINT CLOUD, June 3rd, 1696.

" King James himself owns that if they had been in Holland instead of invading the Palatine States he would still be on his throne; I once talked with him about it. Yet there is one thing that I have never been able to understand and which I have never dared ask him, Why did he not employ the thirty thousand pistoles that he had in England to

that of William III. whom she was already seeking for a son-in-law.

Doctor Fagon, of whom Madame gives so graphic a description in her next letter, played an important part at Court. As the King's own physician he knew a great deal of what went on. His curious diary, which was published some years ago, excited much interest, being the only medical diary of that date which has been preserved. Madame, who intensely disliked all doctors, specially detested Fagon, thinking him "capable of anything." And in an age when poison played such an important part in the history of European Courts, *le Medicin du Roy* literally held life and death in his hands.

To the Electress Sophia.

"Port Royal, Sunday, July 15th, 1696.

"All that is being said as to the other world is incomprehensible to me. *Metemssycosus* would not displease me, provided one could recollect what one had already been previously. . . . .

"Doctor Fagon is a character of which it is difficult to give you an idea. His legs are as thin as those of a bird, his mouth is filled with black teeth, his large lips cause his mouth to have habitually a pouting expression; he has sunken eyes, dark yellow skin, a long face, and looks as spiteful as he is in reality. But he is very intelligent and polite. By this description you may see how

difficult it is to gain an idea of this personage. I
hope with all my heart that what the Duchesse of
Ostfriesland wrote you may come to pass, namely,
that a general peace will be declared, and that my
daughter will wed the Duc de Lorraine, for by
what I observe she would be happier with this
Duke than with the King of Germany. . . . ."

To the RAUGRAVINE LOUISE.

"SAINT CLOUD, July 22nd, 1696.

"My very dear Louise,—I learnt last evening by
the *Gazette de Hollande* that Almighty God has
seen fit to call Caroline to Himself. Believe me, I
feel all the gravity of this loss, and I grieve for
you from the bottom of my heart. I can imagine
the trouble this sad event must have thrown you
into. May the All-powerful God console you, and
send you many joys when your grief is ended. . . .
I only beg of you to send the enclosed letter to the
Duke of Schomberg. I am writing to him in
French, not knowing how to treat him in German,
nor what title to name him by.

"Remain assured of all the affection I bear to
you all; you would certainly not doubt of it if
you had witnessed all the tears I shed on hearing
of Caroline's death. Present also my sympathies
to Charles Maurice and embrace him for me."

To the ELECTRESS SOPHIA.

"SAINT CLOUD, July 26th, 1696.

"They were saying the other day at Saint Ger-

mains before the little English Princess that the
Duc de Bourgogne is to wed the Princess of Savoy.
The good child began crying bitterly, exclaiming
that she had always believed that the Duc de
Bourgogne would wed none but herself, and that
if he was really going to wed a Princess of Savoy
she would never marry, but retire into a convent.
Since she has been told the news she has remained
mournful and cannot be consoled. . . . ."

The little English Princess here mentioned was
Louisa Stuart, James II.'s favourite child, and the
only daughter of Mary of Modena. She was born
at Saint Germains, and never saw England, for she
died at the age of twenty-one, much regretted by
all the members of the French royal family, to
whom she had endeared herself by her sweetness
and kindliness of heart. A charming portrait, now
in the small gallery of Versailles, shows us the little
English Princess playing with her brother at hide-
and-seek in the gardens of the chateau.

"SAINT CLOUD, Sunday morning, July 29th, 1696.

"It is easy for you to understand that I hope
with all my heart for my daughter's marriage
with the King of the Romans,* but I hear that
the Emperor is far from desiring it, and I much
doubt whether our King will really bestir himself;
for by what I am told the old wretch has still the

* King of Germany.

dirty little beggar * in her mind, and wishes my daughter to wed him. But this would not suit me, so I should be very glad could she soon marry the King of the Romans and put an end to this annoyance. . . . . . I doubt whether the Princess of Savoy will be happy here, for the Duc de Bourgogne is horribly reserved and ill-tempered; and she is certain to fall into the hands of bigotted old women, who will disapprove of any pleasures or happiness that she may be given. . . . ."

"Port Royal, Aug. 2nd, 1696.

"M. Helmont's opinion cannot make any impression upon me, for I cannot figure the soul to myself or understand how it can pass into another body. If I reasoned according to my humble judgment, I should be more inclined to think that when we die all disappears, that nothing remains of what we were, and that each element of which we were composed flies off to form part of another whole. . . . . . It seems to me that only Divine grace can persuade us that the soul is immortal, for the idea does not naturally present itself to our minds. . . . ."

To the Raugravine Louise.
"Saint Cloud, Aug. 12th, 1696.

"Would that we all could meet our end as Caroline has done. I think that she died with real courage. Whoever can truly believe in a future

* Duc du Maine.

life is certainly happy, for it is not in this world that one must seek consolation or joy; neither are those called away the first the least fortunate. It seems to me that we, the children of His Highness, the late Elector, cannot boast of having been happy in this world. I hope to God that we shall enjoy eternal life! . . .

"P.S. You would render me a service by sending me the stockings and pins that our late Caroline ordered for me. Write and tell me the price. I also owed her for a pair of stockings; she never told me what they had cost her. . . . ."

To the Electress Sophia.
"Versailles, Sept. 20th, 1696.

"The Prince of Wales is the nicest child in the world; he knows French now, and talks willingly. He is neither like his father or mother, but bears a great resemblance to all the portraits of the late King of England,* his uncle; and I feel sure that if the English could see this child they could not doubt that he is a member of the royal family. . ."

"Fontainebleau, Oct. 30th, 1696.

"I beg of you to thank M. Leibnitz from me. I think that he has written his theory very well, and I admire the clearness and ease with which he expounds so difficult a subject. It is a great consolation for me to know that animals do not entirely perish, on account of my dear little dogs. . . ."

* Charles II.

hardly looks at my son and myself; but as soon
as she sees Mme. de Maintenon she smiles and runs
to meet her; equally when she perceives the Princesse de Conti. By this you can see how politic
she is already. Those who speak with her say that
she is very intelligent. She takes the full rank of
Duchesse de Bourgogne, but she is generally styled
'the Princess.' She dines alone, not with the
King. The whole world is returning to childhood
here; the day before yesterday the Princesse d'Harcourt and Mme. de Pontchartrin played at 'blind
man's buff.' Yesterday it was the turn of Monsieur, the Dauphin, the Prince and Princesse de
Conti and myself. (What do you think of the
company?) To tell the truth I was not sorry to
move about a little. . . . ."

"At PORT ROYAL, Nov. 14th, 1696.

" I find that many things are spoilt in this life
by religion—specially since my daughter cannot
wed King William. I cannot blame this King
for not wishing to re-marry, for matrimony is a
great plague, and one cannot be always sure that
it will turn out a good thing each time. . . . ."

"PARIS, Nov. 25th, 1696.

" No doubt you have heard by now how our
little new Princess was received, and that she has
been given the full rank of a Duchesse de Bourgogne, although she does not yet bear the title.
Since she is to have precedence over me, it

G

matters little whether it is to be now or a year later. With the exception of having precedence over the other Princesses I never had any joy or honour in being first. . . . The passion that the King has for that woman * is incredible. Every one in Paris says that as soon as peace is concluded the marriage will be declared, and that the lady will assume rank. This is another reason why I should esteem myself fortunate in having no longer precedence; at least, I shall walk behind some one who is worthy, and I shall not be obliged to hand the chemise and gloves to this lady. If it is to be done, I wish it were all over, for then there would again be a Court· · · · ·

"I do not know whether the Duchesse de Bourgogne will be more fortunate than the Dauphiness, the Grand-Duchesse, and myself. When we first arrived we also were thought wonderful, one after the other, but they soon got tired of us. But then, we had not the advantage of everyone wishing to stand well at Court being obliged to behave well to us, which is the case with this little Princess. · · · ·

"It is impossible to be more politic than she is,—they say that her father brought her up to be so. She is not at all stupid, and I do not think her as ugly as the others. She is certainly intelligent, one can see that in her eyes. · · · ·"

* Mme. de Maintenon.

"VERSAILLES, Dec. 16th, 1696.

"The *fiancée* of the Duc de Bourgogne is kept greatly shut up; the King has forbidden us to ever mention the opera, the play, or gambling before her; I am quite sorry for the poor child. · · · · ."

"VERSAILLES, Jan. 2nd, 1697.

"By what I remember, King James used to pass as being brave and firm, but never for being clever. I can remember Mme. de Fiennes saying to me, 'The King of England is very witty and agreeable, but feeble in character; the Duke of York is courageous and fierce, but perishingly dull, and uninteresting in conversation.'"

Madame's religious theories and opinions must have greatly shocked her contemporaries. She went through every phase of religious thought. Almost entirely unbelieving at one time of her life, she returned to the early catechism of Heidelburg as the best rule to follow before her death. But she inherited her father's breadth of view as regarded other people's opinions, and she had friends amongst Jesuits, Jansenists, Huguenots, and nuns; whilst she was always ready to discuss with interest any new theory proposed to her by her friends or enemies. Through her letters one can follow every variation, for Madame constantly alluded to religion, and some of the bitterness she felt against Mme. de Maintenon may be attributed to the latter's intense though narrow piety.

To the Raugravine Louise.
"Versailles, Jan. 22nd, 1697.

"It is a very unfortunate thing that the clergy try to set Christians against one another. If they followed my advice the three Christian religions should join together and become one, and not trouble us as to what each thought individually, and only care as to whether all lived according to the law of the Gospel—those who led evil lives would then alone be rebuked by the preachers. Christians ought also to be allowed to contract marriage together in any church without being blamed by their fellows. If all this were done they would be more united than they are now.

"I think so highly of King William that I could rather have him for a son-in-law than the Emperor of Germany. I can truly say that my daughter never thinks of coquetry or gallantry, so from those things I have nothing to fear; she is not handsome, but full of good feeling, and very amiable. I feel sure that she will remain an old maid, for I fancy that your King will wed the Princess of Denmark; the Emperor, a Princess of Savoy; and the Duc de Lorraine, the Emperor's daughter. In that case there will be no one left for my daughter. . . . ."

"Versailles, Feb. 18th, 1697.

"You were right not to visit the Princess of Denmark* if she refused to bow to you. She is

* Afterwards Queen Anne.

foolish to be so proud, for her mother came of a rank far below yours.

"It will produce a good effect abroad to hear that you refused to give up in England the honours that you considered as due to you. . . . ."

"Paris, March 14th, 1697.

"I feel sure that my daughter is going to remain an old maid—at least it seems so. No doubt your King* will wed the Princess of Denmark. . . . . The Plenipotentiaries have gone to Holland. We shall soon know whether or not they have done anything. I do not think that a man could now be found who does not hold King William in esteem; I, for my part, never made any secret of my feeling for him. . . . ."

"Versailles, March 17th, 1697.

"As far as I can understand, the great English nobles come from a stock as mixed as do our Dukes here, there are barely two or three who can boast of four quarterings. . . . .

"I did not know that music figured in English plays, with the exception of the orchestra performing between the acts. Going to the theatre is my favourite amusement. His Highness, our late father, used to say that English comedies were better than any others, therefore I hope that you derive amusement from them. . . . ."

* King William.

"I wish that you could give me more details of the ceremony at which you assisted at Windsor, for such topics, indifferent in themselves, are a great help in conversations. I often find that I have nothing left to say. . . . .

"If you understood the state of things here, you would not wonder at my lack of gaiety. Any one else in my place, who was not of a fundamentally cheerful nature, would have died of grief long ago, but I only wax fat on my troubles. I see few people, and live apart 'like a free burg.' I cannot claim four friends in the whole of France."

Among Madame's "four friends" must be reckoned, Fraulein von Rathsamhausen, whom she brought with her from Germany. This worthy lady lived with her mistress for more than forty years, notwithstanding Monsieur's constant efforts to make her return to her own country. She always remained a true German *hausfrau*, and never even learnt the French language. Madame was greatly attached to this worthy lady, and often refers to her in her letters to the Raugravine Louise.

Early in the spring of 1697, Madame had a bad accident whilst riding at a wolf-hunt. Her horse stumbled and she fell heavily on to the ground, putting out her elbow. On being taken to the nearest village, the Dauphin, who was with her, was told that a very skilful bonesetter, famous for

again. And if he does so, the English Parliament would not allow him to wed a Catholic, and a Frenchwoman . . . . . I always said to myself that there would be no difficulty made as to recognising him King. He has a right to the title, and since a long time everyone here says 'King William.' . . . ."

"SAINT CLOUD, Aug. 15th, 1697.

"Last Monday I was dining with my aunt at Maubuisson. At first she seemed silent and absent-minded. I feared that she was not well, but in the afternoon she became quite gay. We began to build castles in the air; I only wished for one thing, namely, that my daughter should become Queen of England, and that King William should take her to the Hague; then, that you should meet me there, and that we should spend some time together, you and I. Alas! I know that it cannot be, yet I like to speak as if it could come to pass. But my aunt, the Abbess, and I talked together in a low voice; she had warned me that the nuns believed that I had come to Maubuisson to be consoled because my daughter was going to be married to a Huguenot. They would there-fore have been terribly scandalised had they heard how much I desired the thing. . . . ."

TO THE RAUGRAVINE LOUISE.
"SAINT CLOUD, Sept. 4th, 1697.

" It is indeed true that to live single is to choose the better part; the best of husbands is

good for nothing. Amelia's* reflections made me laugh heartily—they certainly would be true if our marrying only depended on ourselves, and if we had our entire personal freedom ; but I am convinced that all is settled by Fate, and that we are not free to act as we wish. . . . . Love in marriage is no longer the fashion; married folk who love one another are thought ridiculous. . . . ."

TO THE ELECTRESS SOPHIA.
"SAINT CLOUD, Sept. 15th, 1697.

" I love this child (the Prince of Wales†) with all my heart. It is impossible to see him and not love him. He is very good, and will in time I think become a great king, for, although he is only nine years old, I feel sure that he would even now be able to govern better than his father. . . . ."

"PARIS, Nov. 3rd, 1697.

"The Prince de Conti will divert the Poles when they see him drunk, for he is very funny when in that state. He then imagines that not he, but some other, is drunk. Last year at one of the receptions I found him half-seas over ; he came towards me and said, ' I have been talking to the Nuncio ; he is quite drunk, so much so that I fear he will forget all the fine things that I said to him,' and he laughed, sang, and made compliments in the same breath. He made me

* Another of Madame's half-sisters.   † The Pretender.

laugh heartily. 'But, cousin,' I observed, 'is it not rather you who have been drinking, for you seem very gay?' He answered laughing, 'Ah! you also share the opinion of Monseigneur, M. de Chartres, and the Princesse de Conti, who all will have it that it is I that am drunk, not the Nuncio.' And if my son and myself had not prevented him he would have gone and asked the Nuncio where the latter had been to drink. . . . ."

To the Raugravine Louise.

"Paris, Nov. 10th, 1697.

"No doubt you are aware that peace has been declared, and signed with the Emperor. . . .

"I do not believe that there will be war in Poland either, for I hear that our Prince de Conti's affairs there are getting on very indifferently, and that he will soon return here. To my thinking this would be better for him than to become King of Poland, for that country is a dirty and savage place, full of selfish nobles. I see that you care as little for play as I do. Hombre is very fashionable here; it and lansquenet are the only games played in this country. Dancing has gone out, but it may come in again soon, for the future Duchesse de Bourgogne is passionately fond of it. I am in bed; this need not surprise you for I am never well in Paris. . . . .

"I must now prepare to go to church for it is Sunday; after mass the Dauphin will come and dine with us and play at lansquenet. We shall spend the evening at the opera, viewing a new ballet, named *l'Europe Galante,* * in which we shall be shown the manner in which the French, Spaniards, Italians, and Turks make love to their lady-loves, each in their own fashion. . . . ."

About this time Madame seems to have given up the thought of William III. as a son-in-law, and to have turned her attention to the Duke of Lorraine, who was in every way a more suitable *parti* for Monsieur's daughter than the King of England, a widower and a Protestant, could possibly be. It is instructive to note how Madame's feelings about William of Orange altered when she gave up the thought of his making her daughter Queen of England.

The King and Mme. de Maintenon had no time to waste over the marriage of Mdlle. de Chartres, for, apart from settling the King's legitimatised children, they had the wedding ceremonies of the Duc de Bourgogne, Fénélon's intelligent and kindly pupil, to attend to. His bride, Marie Adelaide de Savoie, was far from being a favourite of Madame, for she had been brought up, since the age of eleven, by Mme. de Maintenon, and had always behaved but with scant courtesy to her step-grandmother.

So Madame had to actually bestir herself about

* By La Motte-Hudar. Campra's score.

her daughter's marriage, and what she thought of capital importance — the character of her future husband. In one of the letters written about this time to her sister she says, " Write me, I pray, dear Louise, what sort of fellow is the Duke of Lorraine, and inform me of his temper. . . ."

TO THE ELECTRESS SOPHIA.

" VERSAILLES, Dec. 8th, 1697.

" Your gracious letter consoled me for all the annoyances I had to endure during the wedding-ceremonies.* There was such a crowd that I had to wait a quarter of an hour in front of each door before I could pass through. I had on such a heavy gown and under-skirt that I could hardly stand upright: this gown was composed of gold fringe and black chenille flowers, my ornaments were pearls and diamonds. Monsieur wore black velvet embroidered with gold, and all his largest diamonds. My son wore a coat of many colours, embroidered with gold and covered with gems. My daughter, a gown and skirt of gold-embroidered velvet, the bodice being covered with rubies and diamonds. The King had on a coat made of cloth of gold, with silver embroideries on the side. Monseigneur also wore cloth of gold, embroidered with gold thread in relief. The bridegroom looked fine in a black and gold cloak, a white stomacher embroidered with gold and trimmed with diamond buttons. The cloak was lined with pink silk, em-

* Wedding of the Duc de Bourgogne and Princess of Savoy.

ment and stayed a quarter of an hour without sitting down, then each went to his own rooms. At seven o'clock we again met in the King's apartment. There was such a crowd that the King, who had been with Madame de Maintenon, had to wait a quarter of an hour at the door before he could pass through. In the King's drawing-room we waited for the English royal family for three-quarters of an hour. When they arrived, the King, the bride, and I, went as far as the ante-chamber to meet them. The Queen had on a cloth-of-gold gown, trimmed with black flowers, her jewels being diamonds; the King wore a hair-coloured velvet cloak with gold buttons. Everyone passed into the grand apartment where play went on for three-quarters of an hour; from there we went into the gallery to see the fireworks, which were splendid. Then we went to dinner. The two Kings placed the Queen between them, everyone else taking the same place as at lunch. . . . ."

CHAPTER V.

1698 to 1700.

Shortly after, Madame had the satisfaction of announcing to her aunt and sister the engagement of her daughter to Leopold Charles, Duke of Lorraine and Bar.

Madame's two children were strangely unlike, though both were destined to play so great a part in the history of the Europe of that date; for Charlotte Elizabeth became the mother of the husband of Maria Theresa,* and after the Duke of Lorraine's death was appointed Regent of the Duchy of Lorraine and Bar, her strong individuality coming out in several of her grandchildren. It is strange to think this Madame was the great-grandmother of Marie Antoinette—fated to live in the self-same rooms that Monsieur's second wife had occupied at Versailles during the life of Le Grand Monarque.

The Duchesse de Chartres had an unusually long engagement, the wedding being arranged to take

---

* Francis I. Emperor of Germany.

place in October, 1698, nearly a year after the betrothal had been formally declared. We may be sure that Madame was pleased with this delay, which enabled her to instruct her daughter in the mysteries of German housekeeping. In the meanwhile the question of the dowry was of considerable importance, for the Duc de Lorraine was not wealthy. So it was settled that the bride's uncle Louis XIV. should give her 900,000 francs, and her father and mother 400,000 francs, payable immediately after their death, the bridegroom sending the lady a large quantity of precious stones. Just after the betrothal, Madame wrote to her sister, " What makes me hope that this marriage will turn out well and make my daughter's happiness is, that she is not afraid of the poverty of her future husband. She believes that she will be happy in spite of it."

"Paris, Feb. 16th, 1698.

" I had the pleasure last evening of holding a long conversation with my Lord Portland.* He told me that he had often had the honour of seeing you, and that he admired exceedingly the perfection with which you speak English and Dutch. . . . .

" Monsieur, who, as you are aware, dislikes any one to take notice of me, does not approve of my Lord Portland's coming to see me so often, and as he cannot forbid him to he tried to set me against

* English Ambassador.

him. ' This my lord,' says he, ' only comes to see you that he may get information out of you.' ' That would be more to be feared with you,' I replied, ' who know all the State secrets, but I, who know nothing, cannot be made to say anything, and I much enjoy his company, for he talks to me of those I love and honour ; this cannot injure anybody, and you know, Monsieur, how willingly I listen to those who speak to me of my aunt, my uncle, and the Duke of Zell.' To this he replied nought, but soon after he observed, ' This will much displease the King and Queen of England at Saint Germains.' ' I cannot help that,' I answered. ' I pity them and would willingly do anything for them, but I cannot help esteeming King William, for he deserves it, and I do not hide this from them. I cannot refuse to see the ambassador of a King recognised as such, and one that the King and yourself received with every courtesy, and who comes with many kind messages from the King his master to me, asking for my friendship. All this makes me treat him well, and reply to his courtesies suitably, and the King and Queen at Saint Germains are wrong if they find fault with it.' "

"Versailles, March 18th, 1698.

" Last Sunday my Lord Portland made his entry into Paris. His equipages and liveries were very magnificent. He had six coaches, twelve outriders, twelve pages, fifty couriers, and a great following of

H

would have liked to. It is of no conquesence, for
anything you may have uttered during the time
that you were delirious was independent of your
will, and you have led such a virtuous life that
God, who is very just, would have remembered it,
and you would certainly have gone to Heaven if
you had died. For, as says the Heidelburg catechism, as long as we feel sincere repentance and
sorrow for our sins, and truly believe that Jesus
suffered for us, all our other weaknesses will be
annulled by the passion and death of Christ. So
you have nothing to fear, dear Louise. Still, it is
better to reach Heaven later than sooner. The
world, it is true, is not worth much, but to die is
an awful thing, and unhappily we do not exactly
know what will happen to us after this life. . . . ."

To the Electress Sophia.

" Saint Cloud, May 18th, 1698.

" I am glad that my story about Ninon * amused
you. She can lead the life she likes, no one will
ever say anything to her, for she is one of the Pantocrate's † best friends; they have known each other
for years. Since Mdlle. de l'Enclos has become an
old woman she leads a very good life. . . . . My
son is one of her friends; she is very fond of him.
I could wish that he went to see her oftener, and
left aside some of his own friends. She inspires
him with more noble and worthy thoughts than the

* Mdlle. de l'Enclos.　　† Mme. de Maintenon.

H 2

they were before, but everything is sadly changed.
If someone had left Court at the time of the Queen's
death and came back here now he would think
himself in another world. I might say much more
about this, but there are things that one cannot put
on paper, for all letters may be opened. My aunt
often says that 'everyone is a devil sent into the
world to torment another devil,' and I think that
it is true. We of course know that everything has
been ordered by the will of God, and as He has
settled for all eternity; but the All-Powerful not
having consulted us on what He meant to do, we
ignore the reasons for what we see happen around
us. I have already told you my opinion as to the
clergy who forbid plays, so shall say no more,
excepting that if they saw an inch beyond their
noses, they would see that what people spend in
going to the play is not ill-employed, for firstly
the actors are poor devils who thus earn their
livelihood, and again comedies inspire joy, joy
gives health, health gives strength, and strength
enables us to work. The theatre ought rather to
be encouraged than blamed; you are quite right,
dear Louise, not to make a case of conscience of
this matter. . . . ."

To the Electress Sophia.

"Saint Cloud, Sept. 18th, 1698.

"The Pantocrate is very powerful, but I hear
that she is not at all gay, and often weeps bitterly;
she also speaks frequently of death, only, I believe,

to see what answer she will receive. They *
spoil the Duchesse de Bourgogne terribly. When
driving she does not remain quiet one moment,
but sits on the knees of those present, and leaps
about like a little monkey. Everyone finds this
charming. She is entirely mistress in her own
apartment; everything she wishes is done. Sometimes she takes it into her head to run out of
doors at five o'clock in the morning. They allow
her to do everything, and admire her taste. Anyone else would give their child a good whipping if
she behaved so. I think however that they will
repent in time of having allowed this child to do
everything that came into her head. . . . ."

"PARIS, Oct. 15th, 1698.

. "I do not know whether my daughter's marriage will turn out well in the end, but it has
had a sad beginning. Whilst they were being
married, everyone was weeping in the chapel, the
King, the King and Queen of England, all the
Princesses, all the clergy, all the courtiers, even
the guards and soldiers, all the ambassadors—in
fact everybody was shedding tears; the Dauphin
alone remained calm, he assisted at the ceremony
as though it had been a play. The Duchesse de
Burgogne has at last proved that she is kind-
hearted, for she was too sad to eat, and did
nothing but weep bitterly after she had bidden
adieu to her aunt.

* The King and Mme. de Maintenon.

"Yesterday I saw the present the King gave my
daughter; it is a suite of bedroom furniture worth
forty thousand crowns. Nothing finer has ever been
seen. It is made of thick Venetian cloth of gold,
lined with cloth of gold. The flowers would be
better for a touch of flame colour. The suite is
composed of a bed, a table-cover, six armchairs, and
twenty-four chairs; the celebrated Losné designed
it. I hope that they will think my daughter well
provided for in Lorraine; she has twenty thousand
crowns' worth of linen, lace and point, very fine,
and in great quantities, filling four immense cases."

"FONTAINEBLEAU, Oct. 22nd, 1698;
"A quarter past two in the morning.

"How badly they are bringing up the Duchesse
de Bourgogne! The child inspires me with pity.
She begins singing in the middle of dinner, jumps
up and down on her chair, pretends to bow to those
present, makes the most frightful faces, and eats
with her fingers; in fact it is impossible to be more
badly and ill-brought up than she is, yet those
standing behind her call out, 'What grace! Ah!
how pretty she is.' She treats her father-in-law *
very disrespectfully; he imagines by that that he
is in favour, and seems quite pleased. I hear that
she treats the King with even more familiarity.
. . . . ."

* The Dauphin.

Madame seems to have felt her daughter's marriage extremely; writing shortly before the Duchesse de Lorraine's departure she says: "We had never quitted each other—now we are going to be separated altogether. I cry all day long, but I am obliged to hide my grief else I should be laughed at, for here it is not fashionable to be attached to one's children."

But the letters she constantly wrote to the Duchesse de Lorraine have unfortunately never been published, having either been destroyed by the recipient after Madame's death, or called in by the Regent, who sent to all his mother's correspondents begging them to return her letters, as they contained so many facts injurious to the dignity and well-being of the French Court.

"FONTAINEBLEAU, Nov. 5th, 1698.

"The Duc de Lorraine seems very much in love with my daughter. Would that this state of things could last; how happy they both would be! But alas, 'No tree is eternal,' as they say in *Clélie*, and generally speaking there are always wicked people in Courts only too ready to make the master and mistress disagree. So I cannot believe that my daughter's happiness is assured. . . . ."

"MARLY, Jan. 8th, 1699.
"11 o'clock in the morning.

"Mme. de Chartres died heroically, without fear, thinking little of death, ordering everything to be

settled as though she was about to start on a journey. The Duc de Brissac, who during his life disbelieved in God, and led a depraved and evil existence, had on the contrary a great fear of death. . . . . He made a public confession, and began to preach and declare his great repentance for the sins of his past life. He died in the midst of great terrors. Everyone grieved for Mme. de Chartres; no one for the Duc de Brissac. His own parents rejoiced at his death. . . . ."

"VERSAILLES, Jan. 15th, 1699.

"The Pantocrate has not yet returned me my visit. Does she imagine that one can do every possible injury to me without my taking it to those I love the most in the world? She must get used to this. Let her do me as much good as she has done me harm, and she will no longer find anything in my letters but praise and gratitude. But so far I have only seen dogs lick the hand that beat them; men are not like that."

To THE RAUGRAVINE LOUISE.
"MARLY, March 16th, 1699.

"The two hundred thousand crowns which Monsieur received from the Palatine States he wasted without even giving me a farthing of it, and if any other money came to him from there, he would spend it in the same fashion. . . . .

"Those who marry must expect to have many

his fortune will return to the King as the male head of the family. In any case the fortune * will descend to my son; I have no right to the smallest part of it. . . . ."

" A councillor had been to see one of his friends, and as he lived close to him he wished to return home on foot. He meets a great tall fellow dressed in light grey, who peers at him and says, ' Ah! so you are M. Tiquet ; † I have been waiting for you for some time,' and then shoots him with a pistol, but the ball passed through his hair without touching him. He, thinking that it would be wise to seem hurt, falls to the ground crying, ' I am dead!' The other replies, ' Thou art not dead, for thou speakest,' and darts, together with another, dressed in brown, towards him. They struck the poor man twenty-six times with a sword, four times in his body, the rest only in his clothes. Neighbours run out, and they bring back M. Tiquet in to his friend's house. They hope that he will recover from his injuries. When asked, ' Who are your enemies?' he replies that he has none excepting his wife and house-porter. The day before yesterday the latter was arrested. He must have made some sort of confession, for yesterday the woman was also arrested. . . . ."

* Monsieur's fortune.
† This murder was one of the *causes célèbres* of the seventeenth century.

"PARIS, April 24th, 1699.

"You have seen by my letter the anguish I have suffered about my aunt, the Electress of Brunswick's, illness. Thank God she is well again. I hope that He will spare her yet many years. I would rather die myself than lose my beloved aunt; she is the person I love the most on this earth ! . . . ."

"PARIS, April 26th, 1699.

"Many thanks for the engraving of the Czar, dear Louise. I shall insert it into my book of engravings. I think that the Czar has a good nature; he is only cruel because it is the custom to be so in his country. . . . ."

"PORT ROYAL, June 12th, 1699.

"I do not believe that the King of England is in a hurry to remarry. That Sovereign is certainly, on account of his great worth, one of the greatest Kings who ever wore a crown; but between ourselves, I assure you, that were I a maid or widow, and he did me the honour of asking for my hand, I would rather spend the rest of my life in a lonely condition than become the greatest Queen in the world, for I have got to detest the marriage state. . . ."

TO THE ELECTRESS SOPHIA.

"SAINT CLOUD, June 14th, 1699.

"It is said that my Lord Portland is not going to leave King William's service, but only to retire

"SAINT CLOUD, July 17th, 1699.

"This country is worse than England, inasmuch as all the bad people also mix up in politics and Court intrigues. . . . Once married, in whatever country one may happen to be, one must not be jealous, for it serves no purpose. One must lead a good life oneself, and wash one's hands of the rest; but then one has no pleasures in life, and may spend long dull hours. . . . I do not trouble myself as to the way the world is going. I am beginning to despise it, and care little for its society. Nothing has been heard of lately but tragedies; five women have just been tried and condemned for murdering their husbands; others have committed suicide.

"Nothing can be becoming rarer here than Christian faith; they are not ashamed of any vice. If the King punished all those that are vicious as they deserve, he would be left without Princes, nobles, or courtiers, and every great house in France would be plunged into mourning."

"FONTAINEBLEAU, Oct. 1st, 1699.

"I am indeed grieved to hear of Charles Maurice's bad conduct. If he behaves in this manner we shall not remain friends long. I am very angry to hear that he is dead drunk nearly all day long; it is a shameful thing. If I thought that it would make any difference I would write and tell him what I thought of it. Whence comes this habit of his? Papa was never drunk in his life. I am bitterly sorry that the only remaining

CHAPTER VI.

1700 TO 1702.

TO THE RAUGRAVINE LOUISE.

"MARLY, 21st Jan., 1700.

"It is really quite true that the Sultan of Morocco has asked the Princesse de Conti in marriage, but the King instantly refused to hear of such a thing. The Princess was exceedingly beautiful before she had the small-pox, but this illness greatly changed her; she still has her perfect figure, and dances admirably. I never saw a portrait of her which resembled her. . . . ."

"VERSAILLES, April 23rd, 1700.

"The old lady, who is in great favour, detests me as though I was the devil, and opposes me in everything. This woman is also a pitiless enemy of the Huguenots . . . . .

"My daughter is in great grief from the loss of her little boy; she has also had this week to witness a sad ceremony. Her father-in-law left orders to his son in his will to take up his body as soon as he had regained possession of the Duchy of

Lorraine, and bury it at Nancy. Thus the grandfather and little grandson were laid to rest together. This is a sad thing; my poor daughter is much to be pitied. This proves that no one is completely happy in this life, for she is, thank God, in other ways the happiest woman in the world."

Madame had been looking forward to paying her daughter a visit in Lorraine during the course of the winter, but a trifling question of etiquette, raised by the Duc de Lorraine, caused her to be disappointed. The Duc declared that he had the right to sit in the presence of his mother-in-law in an armchair, by permission of the Emperor of Germany. Louis XIV., hearing of the affair, had the Duc de Lorraine informed that the Emperor of Germany could do as he liked in his own Court, but that at Versailles things were managed differently. For instance, in Germany, Cardinals were allowed to seat themselves in armchairs in the Royal presence; in France they were not even allowed to sit down before the King.

Then Monsieur joined in the discussion, and recalled that the old Duc de Lorraine, whose daughter had wedded Gaston d'Orléans, had never sat on anything higher than a stool before his own son-in-law. Madame all this time was waiting anxiously to know whether or not she was going to be allowed to visit her daughter. At last the King decided that the Duc de Lorraine might sit down in a high-backed chair before his father or

mother-in-law. But to this the Duc would not consent, declaring that, having been raised to the rank of Elector by the Emperor, he had certainly a right to the armchair.

Then Monsieur suggested a heroic remedy. Why should any of them ever sit down at all? Or again, Why should they not all sit on stools, as was the fashion followed at the English Court?

But the King would have none of this trifling with proper etiquette, and so Madame had to give up her cherished plan.

This is not the only strange case of etiquette which arose about this time. In 1685, when the Princes de Conti went to join the army in Hungary, they were not received by the Emperor because they had insisted on their right to sit in his presence in an armchair, and, though every other honour was accorded them, they refused to waive the point, and left without even seeing the personage they had come to see.

To the Electress Sophia.
"VERSAILLES, May 9th, 1700.

"My son, apart from his marriage, has often pained me by his disobedience. When I begged him not to do a thing he did it immediately, many times before my eyes. When I tell him that I cannot bear to see him mix with certain people, he speaks to them more than before; he once told the King that I was the cause of his bad conduct, because I hate those that he bears in affection."

I 2

"Saint Cloud, July 18th, 1700.

"King James is unfortunate in not having his
true sentiments recognised. We are on good
terms with the royal family,* but King William's
wishes are followed. . . . Our King, thank God!
is wonderfully well just now, and looks better in
health than he did two years ago. He walks a
great deal on foot, at Marly, when he has not
the gout, and this, I think, keeps him in good
health. . . ."

"Saint Cloud, June 12th, 1700.

"You make me laugh by saying that France,
England, and Holland, wish to govern the world
together. It is easy to believe in a Trinity so
plainly visible. . . ."

Now that her daughter was married Madame
withdrew more and more from the Court receptions
and gaieties, but she always managed to hear of all
that went on, through her son, who often came to
see her, and Monsieur, who was a great gossip,
although he rarely seems to have spent an hour
with his wife, unless he happened to be in tem-
porary disgrace with the King or Madame de
Maintenon. He spent most of his time in gambling,
and as Madame disliked that amusement, and, as
he believed, brought him ill-luck, she never saw
him after dinner.

Monsieur was singularly fond of bells, and would

* James II., his Queen and children.

in the German and Austrian interest, and violent anti-French intrigues caused the feeling between the Spanish and French Courts to become very strained. But Louis XIV. had faithful friends and spies in Madrid. These continually tried to work on the weak intellect of the King and make him distrust his wife and her German advisers. He was actually at one time brought to believe that they meant to bewitch him and turn him into a candied orange. Again, he was constantly being warned that he would be poisoned as had been his unfortunate first wife. In the meantime, and with the greatest secrecy, Louis XIV. proposed to William of Orange to join him in a treaty settling a partition of the Spanish kingdom after Charles II.'s death, avoiding thus difficulties and probably wars in the future. William III., perhaps fearing lest Louis XIV. should make a better bargain with some one else, agreed. The negotiations were conducted with the utmost secrecy by Comte Tallard and Lord Portland, and the first Treaty of Partition was signed at the Hague, 11th October, 1698. By this treaty it was agreed that France should take Sicily and Naples as her portion of the spoil, the kingdom of Spain and the Spanish Netherlands be handed to the Prince of Bavaria, and Milan to the Archduke Charles, second son of the Emperor of Germany.

Notwithstanding the secrecy with which the whole affair had been carried out, the Partition

Treaty was soon talked of all over Europe as a *fait accompli;* but Charles II., acting by the advice of Cardinal Portocanero, made a will declaring the Prince of Bavaria his rightful heir, hoping thus to put an end to his enemies' plots, for all acknowledged that the youthful Prince of Bavaria had a certain right to Spain through his grandmother, the Empress Marguerite, youngest daughter of Philip IV. This will was executed in December, 1698, and the Prince of Bavaria died suddenly on the 6th of February, 1699, it being openly stated in France that he had been poisoned by order of the Emperor of Germany.

Louis XIV. now proposed another and a slightly different treaty to William III. This was signed in March, 1700, and assigned Spain, the Indies, and the Spanish Netherlands, to the Archduke Charles, whilst France was to receive Louvaine in addition to Sicily and Naples, persuading the Duke (Madame's son-in-law) to accept Milan as an exchange.

Meanwhile, the German party were triumphing in secret, believing that Anne of Neuburg, who was known to have great influence over her weak husband, would persuade him to make a final will in favour of the Archduke Charles, her nephew. But Louis XIV., aided by Madame de Maintenon's counsels and secret correspondence, was working steadily for the end which was actullay accomplished. About three weeks before his death

(November 1st, 1700) Charles II. of Spain signed a will instituting Philippe, Duc d'Anjou, Louis XIV.'s second grandson, his heir.

It was thought at the time that Louis XIV. had always had this end in view, and that his offers and treaties with William III. were only entered into to conceal his real design for the Duc d'Anjou. But since the publication of certain State papers and the De Forcy* *Memoirs*, it has been recognised that when the offer was brought from Spain he really hesitated as to whether it would not be wiser to annex Sicily and Naples, extending the French frontier on the Spanish border, than to entrust so great an inheritance to the Duc d'Anjou, then little more than a child. However, he finally decided in favour of his grandson, acting on Mme. de Maintenon's advice, and throwing over William III., to the Court of St. Germain's great satisfaction. And the Duc d'Anjou was proclaimed Philip V. of Spain.

The news of Charles II.'s death did not arrive, till eight days after it had actually taken place, at the French Court. For he died on the 1st of November, and on the 10th Madame wrote as follows to the Electress Sophia :—

"FONTAINEBLEAU.

"To-day I have a great piece of news to announce to you. The King of Spain is dead.

* Nephew of Colbert.

The messengers arrived yesterday morning. They say that the event had been expected for some time, and that his Queen is ill from grief. Our King has been sent a copy of the will. The Duc d'Anjou is named as being the heir. One of the Spanish grandees started immediately with the will to come and ask the Duc to accept the Crown of Spain. In case our King refuses for the Duc, the grandee has received orders to go on to Vienna and offer the Crown to the Emperor. I fancy that the treaty which was made with England and Holland is causing us great embarrassment here. I hear that the King brought the Pantocrate into the Council yesterday, much to the Ministers' astonishment. . . . ."

"FONTAINEBLEAU, Nov. 15th, 1700.

"Everyone yesterday was whispering to one another, 'Don't repeat it, but the King has accepted the crown of Spain for the Duc d'Anjou!'

"I kept silence; but when hunting I heard the Duc d'Anjou behind me. I stopped and said, 'Pass, great King! Let your Majesty pass.' I should have liked you to have seen how astonished the good child looked at my knowing the news · · ·

"They say that the King had him told yesterday privately that he was to be King, but that he was to say nothing about it. . . . He is not so quick and intelligent as his youngest brother, but he has other excellent qualities; he has a warm heart, is generous (a rare quality in this family), and truthful—nothing can persuade him to tell a lie. He will also be a man of his word; he is merciful and courageous, and looks very Austrian. He always keeps his mouth open. I have told him of it a hundred times; at the time he is told of it he shuts it, being very obedient, but when he forgets again, he re-opens it. . . . ."

"PARIS, Nov. 19th, 1700.

" Tuesday morning the King sent for the good Duc d'Anjou into his study and said to him, ' You are King of Spain.' Immediately the Spanish Ambassador and all the Spaniards here came in and threw themselves at their new Sovereign's feet and kissed his hand, one after the other, placing themselves behind him. After this the King led the young King of Spain to where all the Court was assembled and said, ' Messieurs, salute the King of Spain ! ' . . . . "

In the following letter to her sister Madame gives a curious account of how one week of her existence was passed in the winter of 1700 :—

"VERSAILLES, March 8th.

" On Sunday we had a long sermon, and I wrote to my aunt, the Electress of Brunswick ; Monday I went wolf-hunting with Monseigneur, but we did not find ; Tuesday we attended a stag-hunt in the forest of St. Germains, and in the evening went to the play ; Wednesday I wrote to Louvaine and

strong. She is said to drink too many hot wines.
So I hope that our dear Electress will not have to
wait too long before ascending her grandfather's
throne."

To the Electress Sophia.

" Versailles, April 19th, 1701.

" Since his accident (an attack of apoplexy)
Monseigneur is afraid of dying. He has become
quite serious, and has sent away his actress. He
makes her an allowance of a thousand pistoles, and
she will leave the theatre at the time of the Jubilee.
I am sorry for this, as she is an excellent actress.

" I hear that the King of Spain has taken
Télémaque as model. I daresay that he will find a
Minerva in time who will govern him and Spain
entirely. The Duc de Berri is as merry as
ever, and troubles himself about nothing. The
Duchesse de Burgogne is very intelligent; but
she is what any other young girl would be who
had been allowed entire liberty of action—vain and
frivolous. . . ."

To the Raugravine Louise.

" Port Royal, May 15th, 1701.

" All my life I have regretted being a woman,
and, to tell the truth, it would have suited me
better to have become Elector than Madame. I
should not have taxed the poor people as does the
present Elector,* and I should have allowed freedom of worship to all Faiths. I should even prefer

* Of the Palatinate.

This was evidently meant as a gentle hint as to Madame's widowed vocation. Among her "relatives" figure Saint Monica, mother of Saint Augustine! but Madame did not follow the good nun's advice.

To the Electress Sophia.

"Versailles, June 12th, 1701.

"Monsieur was still hale and hearty last Wednesday morning. He went to Marly and dined with the King. After dinner he went to St. Germains, coming back here at six o'clock. He was in a very good temper, and told us about the company he had met at the Queen of England's. Towards nine o'clock I was told that supper was ready, but I could eat nothing, feeling feverish. Monsieur said to me, 'I am going to supper; I shall not do like you, for I am very hungry,' and then he went to table. Half an hour after I heard a great noise. Mme. de Ventadour entered my apartment, as pale as death. 'Monsieur feels ill,' says she. I immediately ran into his room; he recognised me, but could not speak plainly enough to be understood. I could only make out these words, 'You are ill; go away.' He was bled three times, given eleven ounces of emetics, Schaffhouse water, and two bottles of English drops. But nothing was of any good. Towards six o'clock in the morning they saw that the end was approaching, and forced me to leave the room. I was in a

his favour.' She advised me to speak openly to
him. I followed this counsel. The King embraced
me, begged me to forget the past, and promised
me his affection in the future. He also laughed
when I said to him in the most natural fashion,
' If I did not love you I should not so have hated
Mme. de Maintenon when I thought that she injured
me with you.'

" So all ended happily . . . .

" I shall spend another sad day, for at three
o'clock the King will go back to Versailles to open
Monsieur's will. . . . ."

The following passages in a letter written to
Madame de Maintenon immediately after Monsieur's death, and when Madame probably felt a
real fear of being exiled to Montargis, throw a
strange light on her character :—

"This Wednesday, July 1st,
"At eleven o'clock in the morning.

" Had I not been employed, madame, in the
sad task of looking over Monsieur's papers and
boxes, which made me quite faint, so violent were
the perfumes contained therein, you should have
had news of me before; but I cannot express to
you how touched I was by the King's kindness to
my son yesterday ; as I know that this is owing
to your advice, madame, I beg to assure you of my
thanks and friendship, and I pray of you to continue your good counsel. Rest assured that my

the mistake of recognising his son, the Pretender, as King of England. By doing this he broke the Treaty of the Peace of Ryswick, and greatly incensed William III.

The old question of the Spanish Succession came up again, and a Treaty of Alliance was signed at the Hague between England, Holland, Germany, and the Elector Palatine, for the purpose of upholding William III. and preventing the ultimate union of the crowns of France and Spain in the person of the same Prince.

Madame began by having a secret sympathy for the "Grand Alliance," but as time went on she became quite French in feeling.

To the Electress Sophia.
"Fontainebleau, Sept. 28th, 1701.

"You were quite right in guessing that King James's last discourse to his son was about religion. He told him to endure death rather than give up his Faith . . . . .

"You can hardly believe how foolish people are in Paris. Everyone wishes to pass as being able to call up the spirits of the dead, and indulge in other devilish tricks; in fact, they are becoming mad. You are quite right in saying that these insane practices are the outcome of the thirst for luxury and wealth . . . . ."

To the Raugravine Louise.
"Versailles, Oct. 12th, 1701.

"The death of King James has quite saddened

K 2

me. His widow's state would melt a stone. Good King James met his death with a firmness impossible to describe, and as though he was preparing for sleep. The eve of his death he said, 'I forgive my daughter with all my heart for the injury she has done me, and I pray God to forgive her; also the Prince of Orange and all my enemies.'"

"FONTAINEBLEAU, Oct. 13, 1701.

"The Queen of England cannot be consoled for the death of her husband, although she bears her loss with much Christian resignation. . . . I have nothing new to tell you. I walk out here a little, I read, I write, and sometimes the King drives me to the hunt. . . . Twice a week there is the play, but, of course, I can go nowhere. This annoys me very much, for I must own the going to the play is still my greatest pleasure in life . . . . ."

"FONTAINEBLEAU, Nov. 3rd, 1701.

"I believe that King James is now in Heaven. The Parisians go even further, and declare that he works miracles; but my faith does not carry me thus far . . . . .

"They care little in France what sort of life men lead. As long as they do not rob others, or bear false witness, they are allowed to do anything, and everyone keeps up with them, however debauched and wicked they may happen to be. . . . I have written to my aunt that she spoils Charles Maurice by laughing at him when drunk; it will make him think that drinking is in good taste."

To THE ELECTRESS SOPHIA.

"VERSAILLES, Dec. 29th, 1701.

"I am convinced that you are not so wrinkled as I am, but I do not mind—having never been handsome I lose nothing; and I see those that I once knew as beauties have lost more than myself; none would recognise Mme. de la Vallière; Madame de Montespan's skin resembles a piece of paper that children have twisted about, her face is covered with innumerable little wrinkles, her beautiful hair has become as white as snow, and her face is red. . . . ."

"VERSAILLES, March 26th, 1702.

"On arriving here, one of my son's people informed me that a Paris banker, Samuel Bernard, had received a letter from England informing him of King William's death. This brings you a step nearer to the Throne. . . ."

The following letter, written about this time to Herr von Harling, shows Madame in the character of a truly faithful and grateful friend:—

"The sad news of your wife's death has greatly grieved me, and although, considering the state illness had brought her to, death was a release from suffering, I wept for her with all my heart. . . . I can assure you that none can sympathise with you as I do, who can remember what care she took of me in my childhood; and all the trouble that I must have given her makes me feel truly grateful to her memory. . . ."

Madame does not seem to have been much troubled by the death of William III. As will soon be perceived Madame detested her first cousin George, Elector of Brunswick, the more so that he had married Sophia of Zell, whose mother, Elinore d'Esmier, she had known in her youth, and greatly disliked.

To the Raudgravine Louise.

"MARLY, April 29th, 1702.

"The Elector of Hanover is selfish and false. I have known that this was so for some time, for although I gave him several marks of my affection, he never showed any confidence in me, and would hardly speak to me. I was obliged to force the words one by one out of him. This was very un. pleasant. . . . .

"The Queen of England * behaved in a truly Christian and generous manner on hearing of King William's death. Many of the English had wished, on the arrival of the news, to testify their joy. The Queen forbade them to do this, and speaks of him without bitterness. I greatly admire this woman; she has certainly never done anything to merit her misfortunes. I feel sure that my aunt is happier as she now is than were she Queen of England, for the English are a false and singular people. . . . ."

Madame had a special horror of *mésalliances*, which neither time, nor much experience of the

* Mary of Modena, widow of James II.

thing she so disliked, abated. Her son's marriage to Mdlle. de Blois she felt a deep disgrace; Louis XIV.'s to Mme. de Maintenon a strange eccentricity; and much of her dislike to George I. may be ascribed to his having wedded the unfortunate Sophia of Zell, daughter of Elinore d'Esmier. Writing of the Kœnigsmark scandal to the Raugravine Louise, Madame alludes bitterly to the Duchess of Zell's obscure extraction in several of her letters, for she felt heartily sorry for her aunt, the Electress Sophia, who was necessarily mixed up in the whole story.

This year Madame lost one of her half brothers— Charles Maurice, to whom she was greatly attached. She constantly wrote to him begging him to give up the habits of intoxication to which he had early become addicted; but it was of no use, and he died, to quote Madame's own words "literally consumed by drink" at Berlin, where he had lived a solitary existence for some years.

To the Electress Sophia.

"VERSAILLES, April 29th, 1702.

"I can quite believe that King William died with great firmness, for one generally dies as one has lived. . . . .

"I think that Princess Anne soon became consoled for her brother-in-law and cousin's death. I cannot understand how she can have an easy conscience, after having persecuted her father till his

death. I hope that she will, at any rate, not act
badly by you. . . . ."

To the Raugravine Louise.

("Marly, April 29th, 1702.

"The marriage * of my cousin, the Elector of
Brunswick, has done more ill than good, and will,
in any case, result in eternal shame. The Duchess †
ought more than any one else to take to heart her
daughter's misfortune, for it is owing to the evil
way in which she brought her up that this trouble
has fallen upon her. There are some here who
declare her innocent. . . . . This Duchess was of
low birth, and would have been honoured had my
first gentleman-in-waiting consented to marry her.
Think how ill-assorted she must have been with a
Duke of Brunswick !"

"Marly, Aug. 9th, 1702.

"News has been received that the King of Sweden
with two thousand men have put to rout the army
of the King of Poland, which was twice as strong
as his own. . . . Yesterday we went out into the
garden after dinner to see the two fine statues that
the King has lately caused to be put up . . . .

"Believe me, dear Louise, if we had nothing
to grieve over but our sins we should be very
merry. . . ."

Louis XIV's campaign against the Allies, whose

---

* George I. married, when Elector of Brunswick, Sophia of
Zell in 1682.

† Sophia of Zell's mother, the Duchess of Zelle-Lunebourg.

twenty-four years old. You see by this that long-lived people are not rare."

During the course of this spring and summer Madame had a severe illness. " I was twice supposed to be at the point of death," she writes in September to her sister. But, with the exception of her son and daughter, probably few cared this year as to whether the widow of Monsieur lay dying or was well, for all eyes were fixed on Marshal Villars and the army, who really seemed to be reconquering the place that France had lost the year before among the nations of Europe.

Unfortunately Villars' successes were more than counterbalanced by the defeats of the Duke of Savoy and the adhesion of Portugal to the Allies. We are not told what Madame felt or said when she was told of the way in which Montrevel tried to subdue the Protestant insurrection in the Cevennes, but we may be quite sure that she rejoiced when Villars was sent to replace him, and by his firm and wise handling of their leader, Cavalier, imposed peace and order.

" VERSAILLES, Feb. 17th, 1704.

" One finds few women here who are not born coquettes. They flatter themselves that as Our Lord behaved most charitably to women of their sort, he will have compassion on them; the thought of Mary Magdalene, and the woman of Samaria, consoles them. It is a mistake to think that one gets

gentry, so they continue quarrelling, leaving aside
the most important and essential things. . . . ."

To the Electress Sophia.

"Versailles, Jan. 11th, 1705.

"I know Prince Eugène even better than Prince
Louis; the latter has a long nose, the former one
much too short. Although first cousins, they do
not resemble one another in the least. Prince
Eugène wished to enter into holy orders. If our
King had given him an abbey, or only a pension,
he would have remained here. . . . .

"You cannot imagine the piety of the Duc de
Bourgogne; it is not hypocrisy but really heart-
felt devotion; he is melancholy, and goes about
dreaming. . . . ."

To the Raugravine Louise.

"Versailles, Feb. 14th, 1705.

"I do not know how to tell you the impression
made on me by the death of our dear Queen of
Prussia.* My eyes ache so that I cannot keep
them open, my head also, for since this morning I
have done nothing but weep. I cannot think of
my aunt's state without fear; my heart aches when
I think of her. . . . . Why did not God take
me instead of that dear Queen, who might have
long remained the joy and consolation of my aunt,
whilst I am good for nothing and have lived long
enough? But one must resign one's self to His
holy will. . . . ."

* Sophia Charlotte of Hanover, grandmother of Frederick the
Great and daughter to the Electress Sophia.

to-day, as I could not do so this morning as we hunted. . . . ."

"MARLY, May 2nd, 1705.

"When I choose a doctor I warn him that he must not expect blind obedience from me. I allow him to tell me his opinion, but not to get angry if I do not follow his advice; I tell him that as my health and body belong to me I mean to manage them myself. . . . ."

To the Electress Sophia.

"TRIANON, June 11th, 1705.

·   "I am very well lodged here; my windows look out on the Springs, for so is named a little wood, so leafy that at noon the sun cannot penetrate into it.   There are over fifty springs, forming little brooks, all on an incline. . . . ."

"MARLY, Thursday, July 9th, 1705.

"Allow me to tell you the absurdity they have invented in Paris to account for my lord Marlborough not having given battle to Marshal Villars. They say that he believes in and consults wise men and fortune-tellers. Well, there is one at Frankfort who has a great reputation; he sent for her and tried to force her into telling him whether he would have a successful campaign. She is said to have told him that Fortune would favour him, provided that he avoided giving battle to a general who wore on his sword a knot of ribbons given him by a beautiful princess. Thereupon he sent a spy to Villars' camp to find out whether he had

searching for a certain object with great anguish.
'Ask him for what she is searching,' said he. 'An
emerald bracelet,' answered the child, 'Make the
spirit show us the person who took it, and tell us
what he did with it,' said M. de Louvois. The
child suddenly began to laugh. 'But I can see the
man,' he answered; 'he is dressed like yourself,
and is as like you as two drops of water; he takes
the bracelet off the lady's dressing-table, and puts
it into his pocket with a gold box.' Hearing this
M. de Louvois became as pale as death; he pulled
the box from his pocket, and has since believed
sorcerers and all kinds of fortune-tellers' prophecies."

To the Raugravine Louise.
"Versailles, Aug. 18th, 1705.

"My aunt has announced the marriage to me of
her grandson,* the Elector of Brunswick, with the
Princess of Anspach.† I am glad of it, for I hear
that she is very agreeable. I hope to God that
this marriage will turn out all well!"

"Marly, Sept. 17th, 1705.

"The Count of Zell's death caused me real pain,
for I was sincerely attached to him. I do not ask
after his wife, for she was far from being an honour
to us. . . . ."

"Nov. 5th, 1705.

"Do not imagine that those who are always

* Son of George I.
† Caroline Wilhelmina, afterwards Princess of Wales. To her
are addressed many of Madame's later letters.

CHAPTER VII.

1706 TO 1708.

To the Raugravine Louise.

"Versailles, April 11th, 1706.

"I know that you are too strict to go to the play on Sunday; but to my thinking paying and receiving visits is more dangerous than doing so, for during the course of a visit it is difficult not to speak ill of one's neighbours, and this is a far graver sin than going to the play. I do not approve of people going to the play instead of to church, but after having fulfilled one's religious duties I consider that the playhouse is better than a visit to one's friends."

It was currently reported, and in some cases believed, that a doubt hung over James Stuart's * birth; some said that the Queen's child had been a girl, others that the infant had died, but all agreed that a strange child had been brought into the palace, hidden in a warming pan, and palmed off upon the public as the only son of James II. and Mary of Modena. Alluding to this in a letter to

* The Old Pretender.

the Raugravine, Madame says, "Is it possible that you believe the young King of England not to be the Queen's son? I would lay my head that he is what he seems to be. To begin with, he is the image of his mother; and I know a lady who was present at his birth, not at all as the Queen's friend, but, as she owned to me since, to see that all was as it should be. . . . . and she declares that he is certainly the Queen's child. As the English have a fashion of behaving strangely to their sovereigns, it is not surprising that they have not yet seen many foreigners on the throne."

Owing to the terrible defeat of the French army at Ramillies by the Duke of Marlborough on the 23rd of May, 1706, France had to abandon Brabant and a great part of Flanders. The Allies entered Brussels, where the Archduke Charles was proclaimed King of Spain. During the Italian campaign the French army fared no better than in the Low Countries; the Duke of Orleans was sent by the King, his uncle, to command the army co-jointly with Maréchal Marsin.

To the Raugravine Louise.

"Marly, June 24th, 1706.

"My quiet life will soon be filled with anxieties and fears, for my son starts in a week's time for Italy to command the King's army; he will be over Maréchal de Villars. M. de Vendôme is going to Flanders to take the command under the King of Bavaria.

L 2

"It is to be hoped that good fortune will favour the King and that Marlborough will be beaten. Should the King sustain some defeat through the agency of a woman, Queen Anne will be blameless in the matter, another, whose name I will not divulge, being guilty.† Therefore let us pray for peace. . . . ."

Madame was in great favour with the King about this time, but her fears as to her son's safety drove everything but the army out of her head. News arrived very irregularly, and the wildest rumours were circulated. On the 12th of August she writes: "My son is before Turin, and I greatly fear that Prince Eugène is even now advancing towards him, and will give him much trouble. I am in great anguish about him, and this news which arrived yesterday kept me awake the greater part of the night;" and on the 12th of September to the Electress Sophia: "My son is not thinking effecting love-conquests. Turin is the place he wishes to conquer." Then on the 16th, news of the defeat had arrived, although it had taken place on the 7th, and resulted in the death of Marsin, the severe wounding of the Duc d'Orléans, and the dispersion of the French army. "The last two days I have spent in anguish; although they assure me that my son is out of danger, I cannot

† Allusion either to Mme. de Maintenon or to the Duchess of Marlborough.

bear to think of his sufferings. My eyes are so swollen that I cannot see out of them."

"VERSAILLES, Sept. 30th, 1706.

"The siege of Turin with its sad termination nearly cost my son his life. He received a terrible wound, but since the 24th he has been out of danger. I was so distracted during three days that I feared I was going to lose my wits. I have always said that they ought to set the two kings of Spain to wrestle together and award the kingdom to the stronger of the two; this would be following a more Christian course than killing such a number of men."

Madame was always extremely courteous to her inferiors, reserving her right of plain speech for her own family and friends. Writing to her sister she says: "The higher in rank one happens to be the more one ought to be courteous on account of the example one sets to those who copy your manners. The King is extremely courteous, but his children and grandchildren do not follow his example in this respect. . . . . Mme. von Pullwit shows her wisdom by following Saint Paul's counsel. He who marries does well, but he who remains single does better. This is quite my belief; had my life been at my own disposal I should have followed Saint Paul's advice."

"VERSAILLES, Dec. 22nd, 1706.

"When our King tried to convert the King of Siam to Christianity the latter replied that he believed that one could find salvation in all religions, and that God, who had not made every leaf the same green, wished also to be worshipped in various fashions; so the King of France might continue to serve God as he had always done, whilst he on his side would adore God according to his way, and that if God wished him to change he would inspire the desire of it to him. I find that this King was not altogether wrong. I think that there is still a long time to run before the day of the Last Judgment. We have not yet seen the anti-Christ, and before he arrives I shall have time to have assured you many times of my tender affection for you, dear Louise."

"VERSAILLES, March 3rd, 1707.

"I lunch alone all the year round, but get it over as quickly as possible, for nothing is so annoying as to have twenty footmen round you who look at every mouthful that you swallow, and stare persistently at you. I do not spend half an hour at table. I dine with the King. We are five or six at table; no one speaks a word; all passes as though we were in a convent—perhaps two words said in a whisper to one's neighbour. We are rendered so serious here by the endless plots which one cannot discuss. . . . . for instance, there is a madman in Paris who believes that he can call up an angel where he is. My son, wishing to amuse himself, sent for him, and asked him, among other foolish questions, how long the King had still to live!

This can enable you to form a judgment on the rest. I have yet many things to tell you, but I must stop, for it is half-past seven o'clock. I still have five letters to write, and at a quarter to ten I have to go to the concert. . . . ."

"MARLY, March 13th, 1707.

"I am very glad that my aunt amused herself at Brunswick. Amusement is good for the health, and I hope that it will prolong her life. . . . . It is not wonderful that one no longer finds the gaiety in Hanover that was once there, the Elector is so cold that he turns everything into ice. His father and uncle were not like him. It will be even worse with the Prince Hereditary; he does not at all understand how a prince ought to act; at least it seems so to me from what I know of his actions. . . . ."

"MARLY, April 14th, 1707.

"I do not know whether English religious books are livelier than those written in French and German; I find them all extremely dull, with the exception of the Bible, of which I never tire. I always go to sleep over the others. . . . ."

"MARLY, May 19th, 1707.

"I am not surprised that the Elector (of Hanover) does not ask after you; he cares for nobody; but then, as generally happens to those kind of people, nobody cares for him. He does not pride himself on his courtesy; this is evident to those belonging to his Court. . . . . The late Monsieur never missed going to call on my ladies when they were ill, and not only the ladies in waiting, but the maids of honour also. . . . ."

TO THE ELECTRESS SOPHIA.

"MARLY, May 19th, 1707.

"An hour ago I received a letter from my son commencing by these words, 'The town and country of Valencia, Madame, are at last conquered. It is a beautiful country, full of orange-trees, jasmines, pomegranates, and all kinds of fruits, far pleasanter than the horrible country by which we passed before reaching it. Our enemies have retired seven leagues from here and are going towards Catalonia. I do not apprehend any difficult in taking Aragon.' Nearly all his people are ill; I fear that he will end by becoming so also. . . . ."

"MARLY, June 2nd, 1707.

"When I waked up last Tuesday, one of my son's first valets had just arrived, bringing the good news that the town of Saragossa and all the kingdom of Aragon were taken. I am the more pleased because the enemy were twice as strong, and possessed cannons, whilst my son had none. . . . .
"May God continue to render us assistance."

When dealing with the social and even political history of the eighteenth century, one cannot overlook the importance assumed by the lampoons, satires, and caricatures of the time. Generally written in France but printed in Holland, they were

difficult to suppress, and even when the printed sheets were seized, manuscript copies circulated freely. Madame seems always to have managed to see those that were most commented upon, and to have sent copies of them to her sister and the Electress Sophia. It was well known at Court that one of the most clever and by far the most bitter of the *chansoniers* of the period was the Duchesse de Bourbon, one of the King's illegitimate daughters. In her verses she respected nobody. The King, Mme. de Maintenon—whom she specially detested—the young Duc de Bourgogne, all were pitilessly ridiculed and held up to public scorn. She is even said to have been the author of the following lines :—

SUR LA FAMILLE ROYALE.

"Le grandpère est un fanfaron,
Le fils un imbécile,
Le petit fils un grand poltron,
Oh, la belle famille !
Que je vous plains, pauvre François,
Soumis à cet empire !
Faites comme ont fait les Anglois,
C'est assez vous en dire."

To Madame some other chansonier addressed the following agreeable lines shortly after her son became Regent :—

"Vous n'êtes pas, Madame,
La mère du Régent,
Ce scélérat infame
N'est pas de votre sang,

C'est un monstre exécrable
Que l'enfer a vomi,
Un tyran détestable
Qui se croit tout permis."

Strangely enough these lampoons rarely attacked any real abuse. The state of the peasantry, etc , seemed doubtless uninteresting to the Duchesse de Bourbon and her fellow versifiers. On the other hand the Court scandals both at home and abroad afforded a rich field for satires and epigrams.

In sending the letters that follow to the Electress Sophia, Madame showed herself characteristically imprudent, for her son had specially begged her to neither speak of his correspondence nor show it to anybody, and the Electress was necessarily in constant communication with the Allies through her son the Elector and her son-in-law the King of Prussia.

LETTERS WRITTEN BY THE DUKE OF ORLÉANS * TO MADAME, AND SENT BY HER TO THE ELECTRESS SOPHIA.

1.

" SARAGOSSA, June 5th, 1707.

"Tilly has arrived, Madame, and gave me your letter which I had been waiting for with great impatience. I am not surprised at the way they greeted you, saying, 'I was not there,' but I am much touched by the manner in which you have gone into all this matter for my sake. Although

* Afterwards the Regent.

accustomed to the marks of your affections, I always receive them with renewed joy. There is nothing here to tell. M. de Berwick is expected immediately ; my artillery arrives slowly, or rather does not arrive at all, which cruelly alters my plans. Nothing remains for me to say, Madame, but to assure you of my respect and tenderness, due to you from everybody as well as from myself."

2.

" AT THE CAMP, June 12th, 1707.

" I have at last received, Madame, the letter which you did me the honour to write, by Tilly. Through some accident it went to Madrid, which caused me at first some anxiety, but I have thoroughly examined the seal and satisfied myself that it had not been opened. That of the 21st has arrived, but rather later than it ought to have done. I do not wonder at this, for our post is very irregular. Madame, I beg of you to inform me when you wish to play me the trick of showing my letters, for then I shall be more careful than I now am, confident as I am in your goodness to me. It is not the kind manner in which Her Highness the Electress speaks of me which frightens me, but her praises are excessive, and trouble me the more because I know that anything worthy in my letters is that which comes straight from the heart, that is to say the feelings I entertain for you. . . . ."

3.

"At Ballobar, this 2nd of July, 1707.

"Coche has given me your letter, Madame. I am not at all surprised at what you tell me of that good lady. My year ends as it began, and I find my big English mule * as dull, and against everything I desire, as ever; but there is but one month from now to the 2nd of August, and it is little probable, unless God or the Devil should interfere, that some change should not occur by then. The enemy has finally left Cinca, where they made me waste fifteen days to my great regret. Mequinanca is not yet taken, even a saint would become impatient, and I am not yet one. The post is starting. I give this, Madame, to the first messenger, who will inform you of many things. I content myself with thanking you and asking you to continue your kindness to me. . . . ."

MADAME TO THE ELECTRESS SOPHIA.

"So as to make you understand this last letter I must tell you that last year, when my son was starting for Italy, an astrologer made him two prophecies; he predicted all the evil that has happened to him this year, but said that the year beginning on this 2nd of August would be more fortunate. So I wrote to him to think of this coming year; as all the harm predicted ensued, no doubt the happiness will arrive too. He replied to this what you have just read. . . . ."

* Probably a reference to the Duke of Berwick.

"Versailles, July 28th, 1707.

"Villars is not wanting in wit, and is very courageous, but he looks crazy and makes horrible faces. This man is a living romance, although he is horribly selfish. He is not wrong to be jealous of his wife; she is pretty, has a good figure, a pleasant manner, and is a terrible coquette. She pretends here to be very fond of her husband, but no one believes in it. . . . ."

LETTER FROM THE DUKE OF ORLÉANS TO MADAME, AND SENT BY HER TO THE ELECTRESS SOPHIA.

"Algayle, July 30th, 1707.

"I received your letter of the 17th, Madame, the day before yesterday. The mule of whom I spoke to you is but a donkey; his obstinacy, joined to the ignorance of a Spaniard born in Italy, to whom he gives his full confidence, nearly starved our army, and has prevented our doing anything; but by dint of work I have put a little order into all this. We are going to attack Monea. But I fear that nothing better will occur unless God should extend us his help. And I do not think that the Provence affair helps me here with money or food. If all this ends well I shall believe in the existence of miracles and hail you as a prophetess. In the meantime I am as they say, pulling the devil by the tail, but 'God tempers the wind to the shorn lamb,' and what would frighten another only draws me on. . . . . I have had the Balaquiver bridge mended; we shall soon enter our new quar-

ters and I into my 34th year. I hope to God that
it will differ from my last, but it will be certainly
the same in the sentiments of respect and tenderness which will always be equally graven on my
heart. . . . ."

To the Raugravine Louise.
"Versailles, Oct. 27th, 1707.

" The son of the Princesse de Tarente, the Duc
de la Tremouille, is in great grief, for he has lost
his wife; the doctors killed her as they killed our
late Queen. She had an abscess; they bled her so
often that it burst, and she died in a few days.
My aunt writes me that the Hereditary Prince will
not accompany his father to the army; it is a ridiculous thing to stay with one's wife whilst the
whole world is fighting. The Duc de Bourgogne
and his brother, the Duc de Berri, start on the 25th
to join the army fighting in Provence against the
Duke of Savoy. The youngest goes as a volunteer,
the eldest will command the army. . . . ."

"Versailles, Oct. 27th, 1707.

" We received yesterday the good news of my
son's having taken the town of Lerida. It was
splendidly defended by the inhabitants; the women
and priests came out on the walls and fought, but
our people managed to take the town. The garri-
son and townspeople took refuge in the castle.
The Prince of Darmstadt * begged my son to

* George of Hesse Darmstadt.

allow the monks and women to pass out, but my
son replied that he did not wish to lose the sight
of such courageous deeds, and that as they had so
well defended the town he should be charmed to
also see them defend the castle. We hope that
hunger will force them to give in. It is not a little
honour for my son to have taken a town which has
successfully resisted two famous generals, the Prince
and the Duc d'Harcourt. . . . ."

"Versailles, Nov. 24th, 1707.

" I am ashamed of not having answered you
sooner, but I have received so many letters and
visits of congratulation on the taking of Lerida
that I hardly know what I am about. . . . .

" It is absurd that they wish to end our correspondence in Germany; we neither of us mix in
politics. I am very pleased to hear of the good
town of Heidelberg being so well rebuilt. I hope
that God will preserve it from new misfortunes.
Since M. de Louvois' death they burn less, so I
hope that the town will never again have that
fate. . . . ."

To the Electress Sophia.
"Versailles, Dec. 1st, 1707.

" I shall have to pay a visit to the all-powerful
lady when once at Marly. My nature is not all to
her taste. I am not flattering enough. Flattery
is a difficult art, and one that one does not learn on
the Heidelberg hill. To be an adept in it one
must have been born in France or Italy. . . . ."

"VERSAILLES, Dec. 31st, 1707.

"Villars is not at all in disgrace; the King treats him well and often speaks to him. To ravage and burn the enemy's country has quite gone out of fashion. No part of Italy was ransacked. . . . .

"Marshal Catinat is not in the least a self-interested man. He was owed several years' pay. M. de Chamillart, wishing to give him a proof of his friendship at this time, sent him the whole sum in one lump. But he refused it, saying that he had enough to live upon, and that the King wanted it even more than himself. . . . ."

speak of it, and those with the army are forbidden
to write anything home in their letters. . . . ."

"FONTAINEBLEAU, Aug. 11th, 1708.

"I must own that the fall of Tortosa rejoiced me
to the bottom of my soul, particularly as all the
princes, the Duc, the Prince de Conti, M. du
Maine, and the Comte de Toulouse had held the
thing impossible. The Duc, before the King, said
mockingly to Mme. d'Orleans that my son had
begun wrongly, and would never take the town.
But the funniest part of the story is, that one day
they sent M. Dangeau to compliment me in an
ironical fashion on my son's conquest of the town.
The very evening of that same day the Marquis de
Lambert arrived with the news that the town had
indeed capitulated. I wish that you had been
witness of the Duc's and the Prince de Conti's
annoyance; they could not have looked more
troubled had they been warned that their own death
was near. This certainly increased my joy. I was
also happy to see that the King seemed pleased,
and that this time he does not share the grief
caused to those round him by my son's success."

"FONTAINEBLEAU, Aug. 18th, 1708.

"Thank God my son is not wanting in wit.
He has also studied not a little and knows a
great deal more than the princes belonging to the
royal family. He is so attracted by difficulty of
any sort, that he neglects rather too much the

smaller things of life. The taking of Lerida an
Tortosa was due to his determination; the whol
of the council of war was against it. Then agai
they left him quite unprovided, and he had som
difficulty to get food, etc., for his army; but fo
him they would all have died of hunger . . . ."

"VERSAILLES, Oct. 28th, 1708.

"With the exception of knaves and business mer
no one here can pretend to great riches. Villar
alone enriched himself in the Palatinate. Marsha
de Marsin said to him one day that his money
was goods badly acquired. 'It cannot be good
badly acquired,' replied Villars, 'for the King gave
it to me.' 'The King cannot give you what is
not his to give,' answered de Marsin; 'I should
be sorry to have that to reproach myself with.'"

"VERSAILLES, Dec. 16th, 1708.

"Our Queen of Spain is so angry at the
insolent manner with which her sister behaved to
me, that she sent a message to her by my son,
recommending her to make peace with me; she
also wrote such an angry letter about this, that the
King asked my son what it was all about. He
added that he approved of the advice given to the
Princess as to her conduct with me, and hoped that
she would never more do anything to anger me.
Whereupon the Duchesse charged my son to tell
me that her only desire was to be friends with me.
I immediately went to her and said, 'Madame,

M 2

my son has just caused me great pleasure by telling
me that you will behave more kindly to me in
future.   I also will try not to cause you any dis-
pleasure.   I never intended to do so, so have been
more unfortunate than guilty.'   She became as red
as fire, and seemed quite put out of countenance.
' You took my timidity for aversion,' said she.
'And why,' I replied, ' should you be timid with
one who only wishes to appease and honour you?'
' Let us forget the past,' said she, ' and I hope that
you will like me better in the future.'   ' I certainly
shall,' I answered, ' if you behave better towards
me.'   Whereupon we began talking of other things.
. . . .
    " M. de Vendôme has come back ; he came to
see me to-day, having grown, to my eyes, greatly
stouter. . . . ."

                        " Versailles, Jan. 10th, 1709.
    " I must thank you for those fine medals ; * you
cannot imagine what amusement they afford me.
I spend long days in looking at and sorting them.
Last Monday I bought a hundred and fifty, with
the money that the King gave me as a New Year's
gift.   I now have a gold medal cabinet—all the
Roman emperors from Julius Cæsar to Heraclius.
There is not one missing, and amongst them are
some very rare coins that the King does not possess.
I obtained them very cheap, two hundred and sixty

    * Madame was a great collector, and had a remarkably perfect
set of old medals.

as he saw any one placing themselves before
me he instantly signed to them to go away; this
gave me a headache, a cough, and a cold. . . . ."

To the Raugravine Louise.

"Versailles, Feb. 22nd, 1709.

"To-morrow a new doctor is going to be appointed to my especial service. He is a young
man, forty-two years old, and will be the fourth
doctor I have had since I have been in France. No
doubt he will bury me, for I am nearly fifteen years
older than he is. I do not know him, but I have been
told so much good of him that I took him."

"Versailles, March 2nd, 1709.

"I never knew the times so bad as they are now;
the poor are dying from cold like flies. The mills
have stopped working, and this has been the cause
of many people dying from hunger. I was told a
sad story yesterday about a woman who stole a
loaf in Paris from a baker's shop. The baker
wishes to have her arrested. She says crying, 'If my
misery were known you would not wish to deprive
me of this loaf. I have three little naked children
at home who asked for bread; not being able to
bear it I stole this.' The commissary before whom
she was brought made her take him to her home;
there he found three little children covered with
rags and shivering in a corner. He said to the
, 'Where is your father?' The child replied,
'He is behind that door.' The commissary, wish-

ing to know what the father was doing there,
looked, and started back seized with horror. The
poor wretch had hung himself in a fit of despair.
Similar things occur every day. They write me from
Paris that a young girl predicted the date of her
own death, and also that there would be a great
battle fought near Bethune, that the French would
win, and that a general peace would ensue. It
remains to be seen whether or not this will prove
a true prophecy, but it is certain that the young
girl died at the hour and date that she predicted.
I have also heard that certain Canadian savages
know the future. Ten years ago a French gentleman, who was once page to Marshal Humières,
and who married one of my ladies-in-waiting,
brought back a savage with him to France. One
day, whilst at table, the latter began weeping and
making faces. Longueil (for that was the gentleman's name) asked him what was the matter. The
savage wept even more bitterly than before. Longueil insisting on knowing what was the matter,
the savage said, 'Force me not to tell thee, for it is
thee that it concerns, not I.' At last he continued:
'I saw out of the window that thy brother has
been assassinated in such a place in Canada.' Longueil began to laugh, and said, 'Thou art crazy.'
The savage answered, 'I am not crazy; write down
what I have told thee and thou wilt see whether
or not I was mistaken.' Longueil wrote it down, and
six months after, when the vessel arrived from

Canada, he learned that his brother had been assassinated at the exact time and at the place where the savage had seen it in the sky through the window. This is a true story."

"VERSAILLES, March 16th, 1709.

"It is owing to bad people, and not to the bad weather, that I do not receive my letters regularly from Hanover. This is clearly proved to me by the fact that sometimes they give me letters on a certain day, which letters are not those due at that particular date, and so as to show me that they were opened, they take a page belonging to one letter and put it into another. Indeed they mix them all up so much together that it often takes me a quarter of an hour to sort them. . . . ."

"VERSAILLES, April 20th, 1709.

"What name do the doctors give to Amelia's * illness? She might have made you the answer once given by a dying man to a monk who was exhorting him to be patient. 'Father,' said he, 'nothing is easier than to preach the virtue of patience; but put yourself in my place, ill as I am, and you will feel whether patience is easy to practise.' ·

"Death, dear Louise, is the last absurdity that we are capable of committing; so we must put it off as long as possible, particularly when we are of some use in this world, as you are to your nephews

* Another of Madame's half-sisters.

and nieces. Your nephew does not know me, and probably cares little for my approbation, which he entirely possesses, for I blame his father's conduct to him. There is no reason in being cowardly because one happens to be an only son; and the Lord God can take us under his protection anywhere. . . . . So it is far better for your nephew to go out and see the world than stop at home and only think of perpetuating the family name. . . . . In this sort of case I think that a young man may disobey his father; all the world must admire him for going off to fight, and although the Duke of Schomberg seems very angry, no doubt he is secretly proud of his son's energy and decision."

"VERSAILLES, April 27th, 1709.

"Prince Eugene is witty and clever, but small and ugly. His upper lip is so short that he cannot shut his mouth. One perceives always two large long teeth. He has a rather turned-up nose with wide nostrils; but his eyes are not ugly, and very bright. . . . . We shall know to-day whether we shall have war or peace; I hope to God that we shall have the latter. . . . ."

TO THE ELECTRESS SOPHIA.

"MARLY, May 2nd, 1709.

"Queen Anne is quite right in not wishing to re-marry. From what I have heard of him I do not fancy that she lost much in Prince George. To shut oneself up in a darkened chamber is very unhealthy. Perhaps she does not always remain in it.

"As far as I can judge by the accounts given here, the Duke of Marlborough and Prince Eugene come to Holland rather to make war than peace. We are beginning to think that the latter will never come to pass. . . . ."

To the Raugravine Louise.
"Marly, May 5th, 1709.

"Monday I have to write to the two Queens of Spain, also to the Duchess of Savoy, and wish with my business men to settle my bills and payments. Tuesday I shall receive the visit of the ambassadors and envoys; in the afternoon I must write to my daughter and to three of her children who already write to me. Wednesday I write to the Electress and to Modena, and I reply to the letters that I have not yet answered. Thursday I write again to Hanover, and I sometimes attend evening prayers and benediction on that day as well as Sunday. Friday I write to Luneville. Saturday is the only day I have no courier to send out. . . . ."

"Versailles, June 8th, 1709.

"I am very glad that the Elector has resolved to treat his subjects better. When those that have gone to Pennsylvania hear this, they will soon come home. I also hope that the Elector pleases you; it is certain that had I had the happiness to be a man, and been Elector, I should have given you

full satisfaction, and my subjects also. . . . . I live a very forsaken life here; every one, young and old, runs after favourites. Madame de Maintenon cannot hear me; the Duchesse de Bourgogne only likes what this same lady likes. I have done my best to conciliate this mighty personage, but have failed. So I am excluded from everything, and only see the King at supper. I can no longer do my will in anything. I was less tied during Monsieur's lifetime. I do not dare sleep away from Versailles without the King's permission; so I can safely wish that I was with you in our dear Palatinate. But God does not wish us to be happy on this earth. You and Amelia are free, but in ill health; I am tied, but quite well, thank God! You are strangely mistaken in thinking that we hear no complaints; night and day we hear nothing else. There is such a famine that children have eaten one another. The King is so determined to continue the war that he has sent all his gold plate to the Mint to be melted down into money."

"Marly, June 15th, 1709.

"Many hoped that peace would be proclaimed, but the Allies' terms were too hard to be complied with. Better perish than give way to them; I cannot imagine how they can have thought that our King would accede to them. As says the proverb, 'Pride goes before a fall,' so I hope that my Lord Marlborough and Prince Eugene will receive their due. The latter ought not to forget that he was born our

King's subject. I am very displeased with him for having put obstacles in the way of peace, the more so that he did it from self-interested motives, not for the general good."

"MARLY, June 22nd, 1709.

"Peace is impossible, the terms are too iniquitous. It is a wicked and pagan thing to wish to force a grandfather to fight against a grandson who has always treated him properly and obediently. I am sure that God will find some means of punishing him who suggested this evil idea. . . . ."

"MARLY, June 29th, 1709.

" My cousin, de la Tremouille, was bled ten times in so terrible a fashion that when he was opened they discovered that it had caused his death; he had no longer a drop of blood in his veins. Two years ago the same doctor finished Mme. de la Tremouille in the same manner."

To the ELECTRESS SOPHIA.

"VERSAILLES, July 11th, 1709.

" The proverb which says, 'Better find yourself with lions and dragons than with a wicked woman,' is only too true. The Princesse des Ursins, seeing how popular my son became with the Spaniards, got jealous of him, and tried to do him an injury. Last year one of my son's gentlemen-in-waiting fell from his horse and broke his leg. Still feeling unhealed, he begged my son to allow him to go to Barèges to take the waters On his way there he

passed through Spain. Hearing this, the Princess persuaded the King of Spain to have him arrested as a State prisoner, so as to have my son suspected of plotting against this King, to whom he has rendered such signal service. Imagine the utter falseness of this woman. She writes a long letter full of protestations of friendship to me, at the very moment she is playing that trick on my son. Perhaps I ought not to recount such things through the post; but my indignation is so great that I cannot keep silent about the matter. . . . ."

To the RAUGRAVINE LOUISE.

" VERSAILLES, July 27th, 1709.

" Beloved Louise, I am greatly troubled about your health since I have learnt your misfortune. But you cannot doubt as to Amelia's being in Heaven, good and pious as she always was. . . . .

"There is nothing fresh here, excepting that I find myself placed in a disagreeable predicament owing to my treasurer having gone off with over a hundred thousand crowns, leaving my people and myself without a farthing. I cannot live on nothing during the time that they will spend trying to bring him to account, but it has always been my fate to meet with every kind of annoyance.

" Songs and lampoons against the King and Court are still being written and circulated, but these things must not be mentioned through the post. . . . ."

To the Electress Sophia.

"Versailles, Aug. 12th, 1709.

"Entering Paris by the Porte Saint Martin, I saw every one running this way and that, some crying, 'Oh! my God!' all having perturbed countenances. The windows were full of people, there were even some on the roof tops. Down in the streets shopmen were putting up their shutters, and every one was closing his doors. Even the Palais Royal was shut up. I could not imagine what all this portended, but on entering the inner court, and as I was stepping out of the coach, a citizeness with whom I am acquainted came towards me and said, 'Are you aware, Madame, that there is an insurrection here which has lasted since four o'clock this morning?' I thought her crazy, and began to laugh, but—'I am not crazy, Madame,' said she. 'What I tell you is true, so true indeed that forty people have already been killed.' 'Is this really so?' I asked, turning to some of my own people. 'It is only too true,' they answered, 'and that is why we shut the Palais Royal gates.' . . . . I asked the cause of this rising. This is it. Work is going on at the Porte Saint Martin; each workman is given three halfpence and a loaf of bread; there were two thousand working there. But this morning there suddenly arrived four thousand crying for bread and work. As this demand could not be acceded to, and a woman behaved very insolently, they took her and shut her up. Then began the tumult; six thousand others joined the four thousand first, and they delivered the woman. Many servants out of place joined the crowd, and cried out to the others to come and pillage; so saying they emptied several bakers' shops. The guards were called, and told to fire on the mob, but the latter quickly perceived that this order had only been given to frighten them, for the soldiers' muskets were not really loaded. 'Let us attack them,' cried they, 'their muskets are not loaded.' Hearing this, the guards saw themselves obliged to shoot several. All this lasted from four to twelve, for at noon Marshal Boufflers and the Duc de Grammont happened to pass by the place where the tumult was greatest. They got down from their coach, harangued the mob, threw them several handfuls of money, and declared they would inform the King that although money and bread had been promised, the people had received nothing. The insurrection was immediately calmed; the people threw their hats into the air exclaiming, 'Long live the King and Bread!' All the same, the Parisians are good sort of people to be so easily calmed; although the King is popular, they hate Mme. de Maintenon. The heat being excessive I wished to obtain a breath of fresh air. . . . . On seeing me at the window a crowd assembled calling out blessings on my head, but they began saying such horrible things about a certain lady that I had to withdraw and shut the windows. None of my people can show themselves, for as soon as one of them is seen at a window they recommence their observations, saying freely that had they their will she should be cut to pieces and burnt as a witch. . . . ."

To the Raugravine Louise.

"Marly, Aug. 31st, 1709.

" You were quite right in not allowing a post-mortem examination of Amelia. . . . . Since they have taken to opening everybody nothing good has come of it. . . . . In my will I have left orders that I am not to be opened. . . . ."

"Versailles, Sept. 14th, 1709.

" We lost a battle* near Mons four days ago. There were heavy losses on both sides, and nothing but tears and despairing countenances are to be seen.   Mme. Dangean's son was terribly wounded; his thigh had to be cut off; they do not know whether he will recover.   I fear that Mme. de Degenfelt also lost a son that terrible day. . . . . The Landgravine of Darmstadt is dead, and I do not think that the Dowager Electress Palatine will be long in following her. They had not an ounce of sense between them. . . . .

" I never knew such wretched times as those we are having now. Would to God that a satisfactory peace could be arranged to put an end to this state of things ! "

* The battle of Malplaquet.

Villars himself is very anxious, for five years ago everything which has happened to him since was predicted to him, namely, that he would become very rich, obtain the highest positions, become Marshal of France, and be given a dukedom, but that this year he would lose a battle, be wounded, and die. He is always thinking of this, and it troubles him greatly. It would be indeed a pity were so good a man to die. . . . . ."

"VERSAILLES, Oct. 17th, 1709.

"Marshal Boufflers will certainly not invent gunpowder or start a new heresy, and there are many wittier than he; but he has a good heart, and is a really honest and trustworthy man; his word can be taken for anything. He does all the good in his power, is fearless at Court, tells the King the truth, and is not a courtier; this is why I esteem him so highly. . . . .

"The French allow themselves to be blindly led as long as they have confidence in their generals; the officers are worthy men on the whole. . . . . The Czar * has fine and great qualities, and his actions provoke admiration. . . . . I fear that the Czarewitch is only too much his mother's son; if that be so the poor Princess of Wolfenbuttel † will lead a very wretched life. . . . .

"It is a good thing that the Prince Royal sprained

---

* Peter the Great.

† Sophia Charlotte, married to Alexis, son of Peter the Great, in 1711, died 1715.

CHAPTER IX.

1710 TO 1712.

TO THE ELECTRESS SOPHIA.

"VERSAILLES, Jan. 5th, 1710.

"My son has at last given up his dark friend.
He will never see her again. It has cost him a
real effort, for he still loves her, but he had serious
reasons for breaking with her. Firstly, she was
horribly self-interested, never contented with what
she got; secondly, she treated him like a servant,
even kicking him at times; again, she insisted on
his entire devotion. If her son was not as well
provided with clothes as the Duc de Chartres, she
visited her anger on my son; she used to take him
into the worst company, and the whole business
became a public scandal. . . . .

"My son did well in acting energetically, for the
King had long been annoyed by this matter, and
if my son's enemies had had their will, the King
would long ago have honoured the lady with a
lettre de cachet. This would of course have been
an affront, so all is for the best. . . . . ."

Madame.' 'Monsieur,' I answered, 'no doubt I
seemed gay, for my son had just spoken to me on
the part of your Majesty.' 'I am delighted,' replied the King, 'to have pleased you, and I hope
that this marriage * will unite us yet closer to one
another.' 'Nothing,' said I, 'could increase the
affection I bear to your Majesty and to my son, but
could anything increase it, this marriage would
certainly do so, for it overwhelms me with joy and
pride.' 'Your joy increases mine,' answered the
King; 'but do not mention this matter for two or
three days.' Just then some of my ladies entered
the apartment, so we changed the subject."

" VERSAILLES, June 8th, 1710.

"Our King's countenance has strangely altered,
but he is still a fine and imposing-looking figure,
and when he speaks he is always agreeable. The
all-powerful lady and her pupil have really done
their best for us."

TO THE RAUGRAVINE LOUISE.

" VERSAILLES, June 7th, 1710.

"I have to announce to you the approaching
marriage of my granddaughter with the Duc de
Berri. The King came to my apartment last
Monday and told me that he would declare the
betrothal public the next day. I had been informed
of the matter Sunday, but begged not to mention
it to a soul. Tuesday I went to Saint Cloud to
congratulate the Princess; Wednesday she came

* The marriage of her granddaughter to his grandson.

ful looking that the minister asked, 'Do you bring this child to be baptized?' The Landgravine, with her eighteen-years-old bridegroom, deserved to have the same question asked of her."

"VERSAILLES, Aug. 2nd, 1710.

"I have received a letter from Mdlle. de Malaux announcing your niece's * death. I grieve with you sincerely. How truly says the Lutheran hymn, 'Nothing is of any avail against death, O Christians! for all is mortal on this earth." There is no place such as England for remedies against the smallpox, yet one dies of it there as well as in other countries."

To THE ELECTRESS SOPHIA.

"MARLY, Aug. 21st, 1710.

"M. de Vendôme came to take leave of me yesterday. He is going to command the King's army in Spain, but I do not know how he will manage, for he is lame and can hardly stand, through gout. His wife will feel very sad, for she is said to be very attached to him. I think that the speech he made to her at the time of their marriage must have captivated her. 'Madame,' said he, "I am not gallant, so cannot make you any fine compliment; all I can tell you is that as you have had the goodness to consent to our marriage I will never contradict you in anything; you shall always be your own mistress and mine.' I find this speech really touching. . . . ."

* A daughter of the Duke of Schomberg.

"MARLY, Sept. 7th, 1710.

"The Duchesse de Berri comes often to see me because such is the King's and my son's desire, but she does not really care for me. . . . ."

To THE RAUGRAVINE LOUISE.

"VERSAILLES, Oct. 6th, 1710.

"Hanover must have become a smaller England, through so many English having settled there. . . . .

"I also, dear Louise, cannot understand people marrying again. Evidently one has either loved or hated the defunct. Has one loved him? Then how can one put another in his place? Has one been unhappy? Then how can one expose one's self to a renewal of one's wretchedness, unless one is dying of hunger and marries for a piece of bread? Only in this last case is the thing admissible. . . ."

"MARLY, Feb. 5th, 1711.

"I am grieved to learn, dear Louise, that you have taken to coffee; nothing is so unhealthy, and I see many here who have had to give it up because of the diseases it has brought upon them. The Princess of Hanau died of it in frightful sufferings. After her death they found the coffee in her stomach, where it had caused several small ulcers. Let this, then, be a warning to you, dear Louise. . . . ."

"VERSAILLES, Feb. 28th, 1711.

"I send you a flacon of white balm. I know many ladies here who put it on their faces. Monsieur once wished to try some on mine, but I would not have it; I prefer wrinkles to having grease on my countenance. I detest every kind of shine lotion and cannot bear rouge. . . . ."

"God will punish the Elector for his unjust conduct to you. I wish that I had been asked about your silver plate, you would have had it restored to you. His way of acting towards you is shameful. I also have lost everything; your hair would rise up from your head if I could tell you the way I have been, and still am, treated by those round me. But it is useless to speak of it; besides, I should gain nothing by it, and only be thought fanciful and untruthful, so curious would the things be I had to relate. My wings have been so well clipped, that even were I my own lord and master I could not travel. . . . ."

"A great misfortune has fallen upon us. The Dauphin died last Friday at eleven o'clock at night, just when he was supposed by all to be out of danger. He had a violent fever which suddenly changed into smallpox. The King spent the evening with him, but forbade us to come near. . . . . The King is extremely moved, but shows great firmness and submission to the will of God. He speaks to everybody, and orders everything. He is consoled by the thought that Monseigneur died in a very good state. His confessor assures us that he communicated at Easter, and he died with religious

sentiments on his lips. The King expresses himself in so Christian a manner that it went to my heart, and I cried all yesterday. . . . ."

TO THE ELECTRESS SOPHIA.
"MARLY, April 16th, 1711.

"Until Tuesday morning hopes were entertained as to the Dauphin. The Parisians, who were very fond of him, sent a deputation of herring-women, who embraced him, and said that they meant to have the *Te Deum* sung. 'Wait till I am really well,' replied Monseigneur, 'it is not yet time.' Whilst I was at Versailles, the whole of the Court of England came to see me, leaving at eight for Saint Germains. At nine all was going on well, but at ten they wrote to me that the Dauphin was becoming anxious, that his face was swollen, and that the disease * was specially attacking the eyes. Even then no one was alarmed. I supped, and at eleven undressed myself, and talked to Mme. de Clerembault. Then I began saying my prayers. As midnight struck I was surprised to see Mme. de Clerembault enter hurriedly. 'His Royal Highness the Dauphin is dying!' she exclaimed; 'even now the King has left for Marly, and the Duchesse de Bourgogne has sent for her coach to follow the King.'† A moment after they came and told me that the Dauphin had breathed his last.

* Smallpox.
† It was the custom for the royal family to leave the palace either just before or after the death of a member of their family.

" You may imagine the emotion I felt at this news. I immediately sent for my coach and hurriedly dressed myself, then I went to the Duchesse de Bourgogne's apartment, where I found the Duc and Duchesse in a sad state. They were utterly moved out of themselves, as pale as death and silent. The Duc and Duchesse de Berri lay on the floor, crying and lamenting so loudly that they could be heard three apartments off. My son and Mme. d'Orléans wept silently, doing their best to calm the Duc and Duchesse de Berri. All the ladies sat on the floor, weeping round the Duchesse de Bourgogne. I accompanied the Duc and Duchesse de Berri to their apartment; they went to bed, crying heartily all the time. . . . ."

At seven I got up and came here (Marly). . . . . When I arrived, the King was not yet visible, so I went to Mme. de Maintenon's apartment. She told me all that had occurred the evening before. ' At ten o'clock,' said she, ' there was still hope, but at half-past ten things took an evil turn, and they sent for extreme unction. The King was at dessert when the news was brought him. You can easily figure his grief to yourself. He wished to go to the Dauphin, but we dissuaded him, saying that he would only arrive in time to see him breathe his last; thereupon he had his coach fetched and departed. . . . ."

"MARLY, May 9th, 1711.

" It is indeed true that the King has every reason

for regretting the Dauphin's death. He was a very good son, full of filial respect, obedience, and love. This was the best side of him. . . . .

" The present Dauphin and myself are not great friends, but he is always courteous, which is all I ask. He is more deformed than really ugly, for his features are not bad, although he is lame and hunchbacked. He has fine intelligent eyes. He is somewhat bigoted, but does not preach. All our three Princes are attached to their wives. . . . ."

Saint Simon gives a graphic picture of the Dauphin's death, and of the mixture of feelings with which it was regarded by the Court, who hailed with joy the accession of the young Duc de Bourgogne to the title and dignity of Dauphin. Speaking of Madame's conduct on hearing the news he says, ' Madame, who had redressed herself, arrived, crying bitterly. She embraced everybody warmly, evidently hardly aware of what she was doing. the palace was filled with the sound of her screams. . . . .'

Mme. de Maintenon was suspected by the populace of having contributed to the Grand Dauphin's sudden death, and the following lines were written on the event.

" Ci-gît le Sire de Meudon,*
Qui vécut sans ambition,
Et mourut sans confession,
Dépêché par la Maintenon."

* The Dauphin's country house.

"Marly, June 11th, 1711.

" There is perpetual war between the Jesuits and Jansenists, but the Jesuits are upheld by the King, which strengthens them very much. They torment the others in every possible way; and here one cannot get on better than by taking part against them. As for myself I am sorry for all good people who are in misfortune. Although I have many personal friends among the Jesuits I must own that the Jansenists live in a Christian fashion, and do not deserve to be persecuted; it grieves me also to see those belonging to the same faith treat each other as enemies. . . . ."

"Marly, July 5th, 1711.

" I cannot imagine why there should be such a violent feeling against the Jansenists; it has injured many worthy people. M. de Cambrai * is not accused of being a Jansenist, but of being a Quietist; to tell you the truth I have always taken him for an honest and intelligent man. He is very ugly and has no flesh upon his bones. His eyes are also sunk back into his head, but he converses agreeably and in an interesting manner. He is very polite and even cheerful; he laughs willingly, and likes conversing in a simple, unaffected manner; indeed, I liked him greatly. Nothing is being said about Mme. Guyon. I never saw her, but I have been told that she was a charming woman. M. de Cambrai's disgrace is not attri-

* Fénélon, Archbishop of Cambrai.

buted at Court to his religious opinions, but to his having confirmed the King in his hopes that to keep one's marriage secret is no sin. I hear that this advice did not suit everybody, so the Mme. Guyon affair was taken up as a pretext. . . . ."

"Marly, July 20th, 1711.

" I have always understood that my Lord Marlborough's wife behaved with great insolence to Queen Anne. The latter has therefore done well to send her away. What business is it of Lord Sunderland whether the Queen is well or badly served by Mme. Masson ? * This same Sunderland is a very dangerous fellow, the more so that from his meek and gentle appearance one would suppose him to be without guile. He was for a long time ambassador here; he gambled a great deal, and I saw him very often. . . . ."

" Fontainebleau, Aug. 12th, 1711.

" I assure you that the Dauphin deserves the praise awarded to him. The Dauphiness is also making herself very popular owing to her courtesy. Last Monday they invited me to dinner; no one could have behaved more suitably than they did on that occasion; they even waited on me personally. A dozen duchesses were present and they spoke to each of them."

" Versailles, Sept. 30th, 1711.

" Mme. de Maintenon looks considerably younger than her age, although she has become much thinner

* Mrs. Masham.

lately.   I have not seen her face to face for nearly
six months. . . . ."

"MARLY, Oct. 14th, 1711.

"Last Tuesday I went to see the all-powerful
lady. She told me to send away my ladies. This
was serious; my heart began beating, for I thought
that she was about to scold me.   I quickly examined my conscience, but could find nothing to
reproach myself with ; this is what she said : the
King had told my son and his wife to watch over
the conduct of their daughter ; * he had said nothing
to me thinking that I should do so naturally, but
hearing lately that I had said nothing to her, he
had ordered Mme. de Maintenon to tell me, from
him, that I was to speak severely to the young
woman.   Then she told me what I was specially to
speak to her about.   'Although it will be a painful
thing,' I replied ' yet I will do my best to please
His Majesty in this matter, this will show him
that I am always ready to obey him in all things,
but I hope that His Majesty will inform the
Duchesse de Berri that I speak to her by his desire ;
this will impress what I say more powerfully upon
her.' He did so.   That same evening the father,
mother, and daughter, came to see me.   I began
on the matter in hand immediately, thus, 'My dear
child, you are aware that I have only scolded you
once since your marriage ; I had meant never to do
so again, but the King has ordered me to speak to

* The Duchesse de Berri.

and Mme. d'Orléans both inform me that you will
not receive the Duchesse de Berri, nor allow her to
beg your forgiveness for having displeased you, till
I have joined my entreaties to theirs. This is what
I have come to do.' 'What, Madame,' answered
the King, 'Do you advise me to already receive
Mme. de Berri?' 'It is not my place to advise
you,' I observed, laughing, 'but I beg of your
Majesty to afford that consolation to Mme. de Berri,
for she has been truly punished.' 'Your advice
is good,' replied he with great courtesy, 'and is
worthy of your good sense. I will receive Mme.
de Berri to-morrow evening; you can tell her this,
or send a message to her to that effect.' I made
a low courtesy and went towards the door. 'I will
not make you a long answer,' I replied, 'for I
know that your Majesty is awaiting company,
otherwise I would thank your Majesty with suitable
length for your kindness,' and thereupon I departed. . . . .''

"VERSAILLES, Feb. 11th, 1712.

"No one can feel surprised at the hatred felt by
the Queen of England * for the Duchess of Marlborough and her husband. They have behaved
very insolently to her. Still, I think that she
should overlook this, for the Duke did his duty in
the battles and sieges, and I think that victorious
soldiers deserve rewards, not punishments. Unless,
indeed, that the Queen has—as they believe here—

* Queen Anne.

o 2

joy, and of so cheerful a nature that she always
found means to brighten and chase away his sadness. A hundred times a day she would run after
him, each time enlivening him by some witty sally.
He will miss her in all ways, so there is nothing
strange in his great grief. . . . ."

"MARLY, Feb. 18th, 1712.

"We are again overwhelmed by a terrible misfortune. The good Dauphin has followed his wife;
he died this morning at half-past eight. . . . The
King is in such grief that I fear for his health.
This is a terrible loss for the whole kingdom, for
he was a virtuous, just, and intelligent man. . . . .
The King having a bad cold was not disturbed, but
immediately on waking he learnt the awful news.
As soon as we were told that he knew, we hurried
to him. His condition was most grievous, for the
King loses much in him, and since his father's death
he used to assist at the councils, and the Minister
worked with him. He spared the King when he
could, was merciful, and gave greatly to the poor;
he once sold all his mother's jewels and gave the
money to some wounded officers. During his life
he did all the good he could and harmed nobody.

"For the first time, I believe, in the world's
history, a husband and wife will be laid to rest
together on the same day ! I have been so frightened by these late events that I hardly know what
I am saying. . . . . I feel as though we were all
going to die one after the other. . . . ."

Dauphine died from the measles and the Dauphin
from close air and grief. . . . .

"All the sciences interest my son; they suit his
intelligence. But when he tries to play the fop it
disgusts everybody; the young fellows round him,
ay, his daughter herself, laugh at him, but he goes
on just the same. He is like the child in the fairy
tale whose parents invited six fairies to his christen-
ing; one gave him a fine figure, another eloquence
of speech, a third, knowledge of all the fine arts,
the fourth, all elegant exercises, namely, fencing,
dancing and riding, the fifth that he should become
skilled in the art of war, and the sixth, that he
should exceed all others in courage. But a seventh
fairy, whom they had forgotten to invite, arrived
and said, 'I cannot take away any of the gifts be-
stowed upon him by my sisters, but I shall pursue
him all his life with my hatred, and the favours be-
stowed upon him will avail him nothing. He will
walk in so ugly a fashion that people will take him
for a cripple; I will cause his black beard to grow
so quickly and twist his countenance into such
hideous grimaces that he will be completely dis-
figured; I shall fill him with dislike for elegant
exercises; I shall so arrange his existence that he
will not find time nor courage for perfecting himself
in music, painting, and drawing; I shall inspire
him with a love of solitude and a hatred of good
company. . . . .'"

"VERSAILLES, March 5th, 1712.

"I am filled with compassion for the King; although he tries to be cheerful, it is evident that he suffers secretly. I hope that God will spare him to us. Fears are already entertained as to my son's possible share in a future government. They are doing everything to make him unpopular in Paris and at Court. The affair of the poisoning, I spoke to you of, is being again spread about. He is accused of causing the death of every one who dies at Court, even of having poisoned M. de Seignelay, who died suddenly lately. . . . ."

"VERSAILLES, March 10th, 1712.

"Even you must be seized with terror on hearing of our new misfortune. The doctors have been again to blame, for the little Dauphin being covered with the eruption (from measles), they bled him and administered a strong emetic; in the middle of this *operation* the poor child died. What proves clearly that the doctors also killed him is, that his little brother,* though equally ill from the same disease, was left alone with the women, whilst the nine doctors attended to the eldest; the women attending to the younger one left him alone, only giving him a biscuit and a little wine. Yesterday, the child being very feverish, they (the doctors) wished to bleed him, but Mme. de Ventadour and Mme. de Villefort opposed it strongly and absolutely

* Afterwards Louis XV.

forbade its being done. They simply kept the child warm, and so saved him, to the doctor's great shame. If they had had their own way he would certainly have died also.

"I shudder when telling you of the spiteful wickedness of people here. Although neither my son nor any of his people approached that child, it is being publicly said that he poisoned it, only allowing the younger brother to live for fear that the King of Spain, who is known to detest him, should return here. . . . ."

"VERSAILLES, this Saturday,
"March the 19th, 1712.

"I cannot imagine why my son is so hated in Paris; he has never done any one an injury. The late Monsieur and myself were never disliked, neither am I now. . . . ."

"VERSAILLES, this Holy Thursday,
"March 21st, 1712.

"We only talk of the past in the sanctuary.*
War, peace, anything relating to the present, is not mentioned, neither are the three Dauphins nor the Dauphine, for fear of saddening the King. . . . . Would to God that nothing more serious than recognising Queen Anne and the heirs she may designate stood in the way of peace. . . . . I believe that even if Queen Anne had not chosen the Elector of Brunswick for her heir, he would

* Madame's nickname for the King's circle.

have been offered the crown of England all the
same. . . . ."

"MARLY, April 14th, 1712.

" The King of Denmark is indeed behaving in
a ridiculous manner in attempting to pose as a
gallant. I am sure that he hardly knows how to
set about it. I cannot think of him in that character without laughing, for as he is deathly pale,
he must look far more like a dying man than a
lover. One can apply to him the French proverb,
'The dead are never hungry.' The King treats my
son in a proper manner. This makes me hope that
those lying tales made no impression on his
Majesty.

" My son is not naturally given to drinking, but
when he is in bad company he fancies that he ought
to be 'Hail fellow, well met' with them; once
drunk, he completely loses his head, and is quite
unaware of what he says or does. . . . ."

" VERSAILLES, May 8th, 1712.

" I am indeed glad to hear that Anthony Hamilton's manuscript diverts you so much. I felt sure
that you would like it, so sent it to you. But if
you had known the Comte and Comtesse de Grammont as we did here, you would have been even
more interested. The husband and wife's characters
are admirably delineated. I also knew Matta and
little Germain. Good King James is not badly
drawn either, but I think that the writer is unfair
towards his uncle Robert. . . . ."

Protestants, for he has taken many of them for his servants. . . . ."

"Versailles, Oct. 1st, 1712.

"Our Duchesse de Berri is wilder than ever. Yesterday she tried to be rude to me, but I instantly told her what I thought of her conduct. She came to see me in great state, gaudily attired, and with fourteen beautiful diamond buckles. She looked very handsome, although two patches placed on her face did not suit her at all. As she advanced towards me I said, 'Madame, you are looking very handsome, but you seem to me to have too many patches for a person of your rank. You are the first lady in this country, and ought to have a more dignified demeanour, and not be covered with patches like a play-actress.' She pouted and answered, 'I know that you do not affect patches, and think them ugly, but I think them pretty and mean to please myself.' 'That is owing to your extreme youth,' I observed, 'for instead of thinking to please yourself, you should consider the King's wishes.' 'Oh!' said she 'the King gets used to anything in time, and I have made up my mind to trouble myself about nobody, and to care for nothing.' 'These sentiments,' I replied, laughing, 'will take you a long way. Listen to me, I only speak for your own good, as your grandmother, and because the King has commanded me to do so. Were it not for this, I should remain silent.' 'To

of thing. I find that tea tastes of hay and rotten straw, coffee of soot, and chocolate is too sweet and soft. What I would willingly partake of would be a good dish of Biran brot, or beer soup; these things would do no harm to one's inside. . . . ."

"VERSAILLES, Dec. 22nd, 1712.

"My health improves every day, and I no longer cough at night. I attribute this to a certain drink that they have made me take every night before going to bed; one takes an egg-yolk and boils it in water with sugar candy; then one beats it till it becomes as white as milk; I drink this up as hot as possible. . . . ."

TO THE ELECTRESS SOPHIA.

"VERSAILLES, Jan. 12th, 1713.

"Queen Anne must be well aware in her heart of hearts that our young King is her brother. No doubt you remember that many wrote that it was really so, from England, at the time. Again, the young King has a strong family look. No one ought to doubt of his legitimacy, and his mother is too good a woman to have agreed to take part in such a fraud. She has led the existence of an angel here for the last twenty-four years under our eyes. I feel certain that Queen Anne's conscience will wake up before her death, and that she will do justice to her brother. . . . ."

"MARLY, May 10th, 1713.

"Generally when one marries for love, hate follows after a short time spent in each other's com-

To the Raugravine Louise.

"Marly, May 10th, 1714.

" We have lost the poor Duc de Berri, who was only twenty-seven years of age, and so stout and healthy that one might have thought he would live to be a hundred. . . . ."

" Versailles, May 27th, 1714.

" In one way it is a fortunate thing for me that the Duc de Berri ceased to care for me a long time ago; otherwise I should have grieved too much. I own that at first I was greatly moved, but after having reflected that he would probably have laughed on hearing of my death, I felt greatly consoled.

"Marly, July 10th, 1714.

" I cannot express to you the grief I have been plunged in since my aunt's death, and I also have the misery of being obliged to hide my sorrow, for the King cannot bear to see sad countenances round him. I even have to go out hunting. . . . .

" Alas! my aunt often wrote to me that she thought a sudden death the best, and that it must be painful to die in one's bed, having on one side the minister or priest, and on the other the doctor, who can do nothing for you. . . . ."

"Marly, July 29th, 1714.

" I was told privately yesterday that the King of Spain wishes to re-marry, and that he has sent the Cardinal Acquaviva from Rome to Parma to ask for the hand of the Princess of Parma. I do not suppose that they will refuse it to him. . . . ."

three chapters of the Bible, one of the Old Testament, one of the New, and a Psalm. After this I dress and receive those who wish to see me. At eleven I enter my cabinet, where I write or read. At twelve I go to chapel, lunching quite alone afterwards, which I am far from enjoying, for I think that nothing can be worse than being alone at table, watched by a dozen servants, who stare all the time, and although I have been here forty-three years, I have not yet become used to this country's detestable cooking. After lunch I generally begin writing and continue till the King's supper ; sometimes my ladies come and play a game of cards with me. Mme. d'Orléans, the Duchesse de Berri, and sometimes my son, come to see me from nine to ten. At a quarter to eleven we go to table and await the King, who sometimes delays coming till half-past eleven. During supper no one says a word; afterwards, we pass into the King's cabinet, where we stay during the time that it would take one to say an ' Our Father.' . . . . Then the King bows and goes into his apartment, where we follow him ; there the King talks with us; at half-past twelve he bids us good-night, and each retires into his or her chamber. I go to bed, the Duchesse begins playing ; sometimes they sit up playing in her apartments till the next morning. When the theatre is going on I go there from seven till supper. The hunts always start at one o'clock. If I go out I get up at eight and go to chapel at eleven. . . . ."

" FONTAINEBLEAU, 22nd Sept. 1714.

" I have seen Lord Peterborough twice. He he a singular kind of discourse, and is as witty as t devil ; but he is very odd, and speaks in an extra ordinary fashion.

" I am really annoyed when I think that th old and odious Duchesse of Zell is still alive, whi our dear Electress has departed this life."

" VERSAILLES, Nov. 3rd, 1714.

" The King of England * sent to tell me by Martini that he would write to me as soon as was settled in England. Yesterday M. Prior broug me a letter from him, but not written with his ow hand, but by a secretary. I ought not to fe offended or surprised, remembering how this Ki has always treated me. He is just the opposite his mother. But whatever happens I shall alwa remember that he is my aunt's son, and wish hi every happiness. I am writing to him to-day. am so sorry for the Princess of Wales. I estee her greatly, for I find that she has very good an lofty sentiments ; rare things just now."

" MARLY, Nov. 8th, 1714.
" Half-past six o'clock.

" I do not believe that the English, who are impatient, will put up for any time with a Kin who cannot speak their language. They say th he is only allowed to keep one German servant.

" I live as though I were quite alone in the worl

* George I.

P 2

I shall never see my daughter again. My son is absorbed in his own family, and only comes to see me when others are by, or when I have many letters to write. He comes then so as to avoid seeing me in private. But I am resigned at this state of things. I allow him and his family to act according to their fancy, and I meddle in nothing. I go to visit his wife and daughters as though they were foreign princesses."

"VERSAILLES, Dec. 27th, 1714.

"After dinner I walked about my room for half-an-hour, and amused myself with my pets, for I have here with me two parrots, a canary, and eight little dogs. . . . .

" No doubt your boat was a yacht.* I cannot understand how any one can make up his mind to venture on to the sea. You must be indeed courageous not to have been frightened. Who would not be sick, shaken about in such a fashion?"

* The Rangravine was returning to England to be with her nieces, the Ladies Schomberg.

say? Everyone has his own nature, and it is certainly not at the age of fifty-four that people change. . . . .

"Dear Louise, your brother-in-law * evidently wishes to marry his daughters like the Seigneur Harpagon, that is to say, without a dowry. But to do this is not an easy matter anywhere, the gentlemen being more in love with the fair money box than with the lovely ladies themselves. I am sorry for your niece's sake that she is not going to settle in our own dear country. A good German is worth all the English put together. . . . ."

"Jan. 10th, 1715.

"I have just received the sad news of the Archbishop of Cambrai's † death, which occurred some days ago. He is much mourned, and was a sincere friend of my son.

"A certain Prince of Anhalt Zeits brought me several kind messages from the Prince of Wales, but not a word from the King. Our Duchesse of Hanover, now residing at Modena, is not better treated by him than myself. I do not know what causes him to be so discourteous. But for my not being Protestant I should be in his place, for I was far nearer the English throne than himself, for it is through a member of my family, his mother, that he is King of England.

"I beg of you, dear Louise, to thank the Prince

. * The Duke of Schomberg.
† Fénélon died Jan. 7th, 1715, at the age of sixty-four.

me, for although I have not the honour of being personally acquainted with her, it shows me the affection she must have borne to my aunt. As for the Bézoard, the Jesuits make it at Goa. My son has many boxes filled with it, given by the Fathers to Monsieur. I am surprised that they accept anything coming from a Jesuit, in England. When I told Lord Stairs so, he laughed heartily."

"VERSAILLES, March 12th, 1715.
"The Cardinal de Bouillon died last week at Rome. He is no great loss, for he was as false as the devil, thoroughly spiteful, and led an evil life; in short, he was worth nothing. . . . .

"I pass on to what you tell me of your niece; your trust in my judgment touches me greatly. I must tell you that the marriage you speak of seems to me highly suitable, provided that the gentleman has enough to keep his wife in a proper manner in her own rank of life. If that is the case, and the young people love one another, all will go well; but if he is poor, give up the idea altogether; for as far as I know, dear Louise, love is only a question of time; afterwards comes bitterness and quarrels; and one gets a heap of children, with nothing to bring them up on. In this case, instead of a marriage uniting two lovers, it brings two future enemies together. I have seen examples of this, so I think I ought to give you this warning. . . . ."

"VERSAILLES, April 23rd, 1715.
"They say here that the Prince of Wales has quarrelled with his father to such an extent that they no longer speak to one another, and that a kind of petition was presented to the Princess of Wales, setting forth that as she was pious and good she must be aware that the kingdom belonged rightly to him styled the Pretender, for that he was as surely the son of James II. as that her husband was the son of the Count von Kœnigsmark! If such a thing was really said to the worthy Princess, it was frightfully insolent. . . . .

"Indeed England is a singular country. The people there are quite different from those anywhere else. There is a Genoese envoy here who dislikes them so greatly that he declares that not only would he refuse to go to England, but he would even dislike his portrait being there. . . . ."

"VERSAILLES, May 3rd, 1715.
"After dinner, my little grandson came to see me. I provided an amusement for him suitable to his age. This was a triumphal chariot drawn by a large cat, in which sat a little dog named Adrienne; a pigeon was coachman, two others pages, and a dog as footman stood behind. This last is named Piquart, and when Adrienne gets out of the chariot, he puts down the step. The cat is named Castille. Piquart also allows himself to be harnessed. I have a dog named Badine who knows all the cards, and who brings anything she is asked for. . . .

"England certainly owes much to the Duchess of Portsmouth.* She is the best sort of woman I have ever met. She is very polite, and converses agreeably. During Monsieur's lifetime, we often had her at Saint Cloud, so I saw a good deal of her. . . . ."

"MARLY, July 12th, 1715.

"I should be very glad to enter into correspondence with the Princess of Wales, for I am truly attached to Her Royal Highness; but between ourselves, they are very touchy here as to all that concerns the English Court. If there should come a change, I shall certainly write to her, for all who know this Princess love her. She is too good not to be beloved and honoured by all who approach her. . . ."

These letters, written by Madame to the younger cousin she was never destined to meet, show that Caroline of Anspach must have taken a great interest in the Court and courtiers of *Le Grand Monarque;* for Madame's letters to her deal almost entirely with her past life. It is, of course, possible that with age the mother of the Regent learnt prudence, and abstained from sending news of what went on from day to day in Paris to England, but we incline to the belief that Madame loved to speak of the good old days, and that the Princess of Wales

* Louise de Kerouailles, mistress of Charles II.

took pleasure in her elderly relative's reminiscences of a past age.

Naturally, when her son became Regent, Madame was enabled to write far more freely and to whom she liked, as will be seen.

To the Princess of Wales.

"July 28th, 1715.

"The Dauphin (Louis XIV's son) was not wanting in wit. He was keenly aware of anything ridiculous in himself as well as in those round him, and could tell a good story when he took the trouble, but his great laziness made him neglect everything. He would have preferred an indolent life to all the kingdoms and empires of the world. . . . . What prevented the King acknowledging old Maintenon as his queen, was the good reason given him by the Archbishop of Cambrai, M. de Fénelon, against such a step being taken. This is why she persecuted this good and worthy prelate to the day of his death. . . . ."

To the Raugravine Louise.

"MARLY, Aug. 8th, 1715.

"Once back at Versailles I will have a copy taken of my portrait by Rigaud, who made it extraordinarily like me. You will see, my dear Louise, how old I have grown. One must not be surprised at the Pretender wishing to obtain a throne to which he has every right, and from which his religion alone excludes him. I cannot understand why the English hate him so. He is one of the

best and worthiest personages ever created by God.
I only wish, as I have often said, that King George
were Emperor of Germany, and the Pretender
King of England. . . . ."

" I am so much troubled, dear Louise, that I
hardly know what I am saying or doing; yet I
must answer your kind letter as well as I am able.
I must first tell you that yesterday we had the
saddest and most touching sight that it is possible
to conceive. After having prepared for death and
received the last sacraments the King sent for the
Dauphin, made him a short discourse, and then gave
him his blessing. After this he sent for me, the
Duchesse de Berri, and all his other children and
grandchildren. He bade me adieu in so touching
and tender a fashion that I wonder I did not faint
from emotion. He assured me that he had always
loved me more than I had thought, and that he
regretted ever having given me any pain. He asked
me to think of him sometimes, adding that he felt
sure I should do so, for that I had always shown
him sincere affection. Then he gave me his blessing,
and wished me every happiness in my future life.
I threw myself on my knees, kissing his hand. He
embraced me and turned towards the others, telling
them to remain united one with the other. Thinking that he said this to me, I answered that I would
obey him as long as I lived. He smiled and said,
'I do not say this to you, rather to the other

Princesses, for you do not require such a recom-
mendation.' You may imagine my feelings on
hearing this.

" The King shows extraordinary firmness; he
orders and settles everything as though he was only
going a journey. He has said good-bye to all his
faithful servants, recommending them to my son,
whom he has appointed Regent. . . . .

" I think that I shall be the first to follow the
King after his death. He still lives, but has become
so feeble that all hope is over. I say that I shall
probably be the first to follow him, because of my
advanced age, and, also, because once the King is
dead they will take the young King* to Vincennes,
whilst we shall all go to Paris, and the air there
makes me ill. Again, being in deep mourning, I
shall be deprived of air and exercise ; thus I am
certain to fall ill.

" It is false that Mme. de Maintenon is dead.
She is in good health, and in the King's chamber,
where she stays all day and all night. . . . ."

" I have found it impossible to write to you
before, for I have been overwhelmed with trouble
and grief. The King died last Sunday,† at nine
o'clock in the morning. Since then I have had
many visits to receive and letters to send. . . . .

"I must tell you that I have been very pleased

* Louis XV.   † Sept. 1st.

to see that the army and the populace immediately
recognised my son as Regent. . . . .

" He made a speech to the Parliament, which was
very well received. The young King is very deli-
cate. The Ministers belonging to the last reign will
keep their posts, and as they are doubtless as prying
as before our letters will still be opened. . . . .

" I am glad to hear that King George and the
Royal family are in good health. . . . .

" My Lord Stairs has brought me the two portraits of the little Princesses. Thank the Princess of
Wales from me for her charming gifts. . . . ."

In the preceding letters Madame has given as
touching and remarkable a description of Louis XIV
on his deathbed, as did any writer, then or since.
Saint Simon tells us of the tramp of the courtiers' feet
hurrying away from the dying King, and of the
selfish conduct of Mme. de Maintenon, but Madame
for once saw the nobler and higher aspect of the
Grand Monarque's death, his firmness and last re-
commendation to those around him to agree and
sink their private spites in favour of the infant, so
soon to be proclaimed Louis XV.

The King's death made a change both for
the worse and for the better in Madame's condition. The King, although despotic and obstinate
in dealing with his brother's widow, had always
treated her with great consideration and respect.
In the Regent's Court, Madame, though feared for

her power of speaking bluntly to those over whom
she had any authority, was felt to be a kill-joy and
mar-sport. Still the Regent tried to show his mother
that he meant to do her honour by giving her a far
finer and more important suite of rooms both in
Paris and at Versailles. The little King was established for the time being at Vincennes, and Mme.
de Berri persuaded Madame and her father to lend
her Saint Cloud, which was conveniently near
both to Paris and Versailles.

TO THE RAUGRAVINE LOUISE.
" PARIS, Sept. 13th, 1715.

" I am not surprised at your having felt grieved
at the King's death, dear Louise, but far stranger
things than those I wrote to you occurred. . . . .

"Yesterday the young King was taken to the
Parliament House, and the fact of my son's Regency
declared and registered ; so that is settled. I feel
sure that my son desires me to have every comfort,
and feel every happiness, but this is impossible in
my present condition of mind and body. . . .

" My son has other things to think about than my
happiness. He is greatly in need of progress ; but
seems determined to follow the late King's commands and live on good terms with his family. . . .
I have made up my mind to keep out of politics
altogether, for France has, unfortunately for herself, been governed by too many women already ;
and I do not wish my son to be suspected of being
governed by his mother. I hope that he will take

my example to heart, and not allow himself to be led by any woman. . . . .

"Do not imagine, my dear Louise, that the King's death makes my life any freer. I have to live in just the same manner, for it is the custom of the country to do as I have hitherto done. . . . . The King showed the greatest firmness to the end. He said, laughing, to Mme. de Maintenon, 'I had heard say that it was difficult to die; I can assure you that I find it a very easy matter.' He remained twenty-four hours without speaking to anyone, only murmuring to himself, 'My God, have pity on me!' 'Lord, I am ready to be with thee.' Then he repeated in the most devout manner the Pater Noster, and died recommending his soul to God. . . . ."

"PARIS, Sept. 17th, 1715.

"The Parliament has formally recognised my son's right to the Regency.

"The King had informed him that he would have no reason to complain of the terms of his will. When it was opened it was found to be entirely in favour of the Duc de Maine. It is easy to guess to whom we owe this. . . . ."

Madame here alludes to Mme. de Maintenon, who regarded the Duc du Maine as her own child. Even from Saint Cyr, where she lived retired from the world, she continued to advise her foster son politically till her death.

sion of Bristol. I own that I should be better
pleased to know King George and the Royal
family safe in Hanover. . . . . When one has
attained the age of sixty-three years, one has
naturally one's religious opinions really settled. I
share Saint Paul's belief that it matters little
whether one is a disciple of Paul or of Cephas, so
that one belongs to Christ. I hope, with God's
help, to live and die in this persuasion ! . . . . ."

To the Princess of Wales.
" Paris, Nov. 5th, 1715.

" Mme. de Maintenon has retired to the establishment of Saint Cyr, which she herself founded. She
was far more than the King's mistress. She had
been governess to Mme. de Montespan's children,
but ended by becoming a most important personage. No devil in Hell can have behaved in a more
wicked fashion. Her ambition ruined France. The
Fontange * was a worthy creature. I knew her
well. She had been one of my maids-of-honour.
She was beautiful from head to foot, but very
foolish, and wanting in judgment. . . . ."

To the Raugravine Louise.
" Paris, Nov. 14th, 1715.

" I think that many will declare themselves
against King George, for the Chevalier † has gone
to Scotland. I was told this evening all about his

---

* One of Louis XIV.'s early mistresses.
† The old Pretender.

---

flight. He was at Commeray hunting with the
Prince of Vaudemont. After the hunt they sat at
table till past midnight. Going into his chamber
he told his friends that he was very tired, and
asked to be allowed to sleep till he woke. At two
o'clock the next day he had not yet shown himself.
His servants were frightened and entered into his
apartment. Not finding him there, they ran with
the news to the Prince de Vaudemont. He pretended to know nothing. After an hour's useless
search, the Prince ordered the drawbridge to be
lifted, and forbade any one leaving the Castle for
three days. Whilst all this was going on the Chevalier was making the best of his way to Brittany.
Once there, he embarked in a fisherman's boat, which
took him to a Scotch vessel, where he found several
Scotch noblemen with whom he reached Scotland. . .

" No one knows how all this will end. I am
grieved for both rivals. King George is my dear
aunt's son, which endears him to me as though he
was my own child. On the other hand, the Pretender is related to me, and is the best man in
the world. He and his mother have always behaved
towards me in the kindest manner possible. So I
cannot wish any harm to come to either of these
two Princes."

" Tuesday, Jan. 3rd, 1716.

" Thank God! Our young King is in good
health. He has not been ill one single moment.
He is very restless, and does not like sitting in the

same position two minutes together. To tell the truth he is a badly brought up child. They allow him his own will in everything, for fear he should fall ill. . . . . I hope that God will preserve us from any fresh wars ! . . . .

"Warlike symptoms are showing themselves in England, now that Scotland has acknowledged the Pretender as King. Once upon a time were there Kings of England and Kings of Scotland ? If our King George would content himself with England, Ireland, and his German possessions, he would still be a great king, and might leave Scotland to the other. . . . ."

TO THE PRINCESS OF WALES.

"PARIS, Jan. 8th, 1716.

" There were never two brothers more unlike than the late King and Monsieur; yet they were sincerely attached to one another. The King was tall, had light brown hair; he was manly, and handsome. Monsieur was not unpleasant looking, but he was very short, had jet black hair, thick dark eyebrows, large brown eyes, a long thin face, a big nose, and a very small mouth, filled with ugly teeth. . . . . The King loved hunting, going to the play and hearing music; Monsieur only cared for large receptions and assemblies. The King was very fond of the ladies; I do not believe that Monsieur was ever in love in his life. . . . ."

" PARIS, Jan. 9th, 1716.

"My son has a very good memory, and sees

everything very quickly and justly. He resembles neither his father nor mother. Monsieur had a long face; my son's is square. He walks in the same manner however, and makes the same gestures; but Monsieur had a small mouth and ugly teeth, whilst my son has a large mouth and pretty teeth."

TO THE RAUGRAVINE LOUISE.

" PARIS, Jan. 21st, 1716.

" I do not know, dear Louise, what the winter is like in England, but I have never felt such cold in my life here. It is five weeks since we have received any news from England. This is not surprising, for they say that the sea is covered with ice at Calais, and that English vessels cannot leave Dover. This annoys me greatly, for I am longing to hear how the Pretender's affairs are going on. The Queen of England was indeed pleased to hear of her son's reception in Scotland. The poor woman is not used to hearing good news; it has taken away her fever.

" You are indeed right in observing that my son is just. He is only too good; this leads him on to do many foolish actions. . . . ."

" PARIS, Feb. 21st, 1716.

" I have been told that the Pope and the King of Spain have provided the Pretender with money. My son has given him absolutely nothing. . . . The Pope gave him thirty thousand francs, the King of Spain three hundred thousand florins."

"Paris, March 19th, 1716.

"If doing anything could have prevented my
son's marriage, I should have done it; but since it
has become a fact, I have done everything to conciliate her."

"Paris, April 2nd, 1716.

"My son is no longer a youth of twenty. He is
forty-two years of age, so the Parisians cannot forgive him for running after the ladies and haunting
assemblies and balls as though he was still a young
man, whilst he ought to be occupying himself with
the affairs of State. When the late King ascended
the throne all went on so well that he had time to
amuse himself, but to-day all has changed; they
have to work day and night to repair the harm the
King, or rather his faithless Ministers, caused. . . ."

"Paris, April 14th, 1716.

"I do not know whether it is true that Mme. de
Maintenon had M. de Louvois poisoned, but I have
heard that when he was dying, her doctor was
heard to say, 'I deserve death for having poisoned
my master, M. de Louvois, in the hopes of becoming the King's physician as Mme. de Maintenon
has promised me I shall.' . . . ."

"Paris, May 1st, 1716.

"If my father had cared for me, as I cared for
him, he could never have sent me into such a
dangerous country. I only came here from obedience to him, and quite against my own desire. The
first Dauphine died quietly, being quite resigned.
She was as surely sent into the next world as if a
pistol had been fired at her. . . . ."

"Paris, May 9th, 1716.

"Long before his death the King became really
converted, and gave up all his gallantries. He even
exiled the Duchesse de la Ferté, because she pretended to be wildly in love with him. She used to
have his portrait, even inside her coach when travelling, always before her eyes. The King declared
that she made him seem ridiculous, and ordered
her to retire into her country-house. . . . ."

"Paris, June 26th, 1716.

"I once had a French correspondent in Holland
who used to inform me of the way in which the
Prince of Orange's affairs were going on. Thinking that I should be rendering the King a service
by telling him what I had heard, I did so. The
King thanked me, but in the morning he said,
laughing, 'My Ministers declare that you have
been misinformed, and that there is not a word of
truth in what you told me.' I replied, 'Time will
show whether my correspondent or your Majesty's
Ministers were in the right. I only wished to
serve you, Monsieur.' Some time after, when King
William's presence in England was an acknowledged
fact, M. de Torcy came and told me that I ought
always to tell him of any news I received. I answered, 'You told the King that I only received

history out of his imagination as a joke, but he earnestly declares that he really found it in the annals of Sweden."

To the Raugravine Louise.

"July 7th, 1716.

"Just as I was finishing my letter to the Princess of Wales they came and announced to me that my daughter-in-law was far from well. Knowing what to expect, I started at eleven o'clock in my coach. At a quarter to one I entered the ante-chamber, where someone met me, informing me in a whisper that Her Royal Highness had been happily brought to bed about an hour previously. But this was said so dolefully that I immediately suspected what indeed turned out to be the truth. Mme. d'Orléans had presented us with a seventh daughter. . . . ."

"July 12th, 1716.

"My son is very angry with my Lord Stairs, because he suspected this lord of having injured him in the King's * estimation, and prevented a Franco-Dutch private alliance. My son has been reproached with allowing the Pretender to leave France; but this was not in any way his fault. He faithfully and loyally executed his part of the treaty, that is to say, to assist the Pretender in no way, neither with money nor arms. My son thinks that the English are unwilling to see their King ally himself with France. . . . ."

* George I.

To the Princess of Wales.

"July 13th, 1716.

"Many say here that Madame* was not beautiful, but she was so graceful that everything suited her. She could never forgive anybody. She managed to get the Chevalier de Lorraine banished, but he got rid of her son. He sent the poison from Italy by a man named Moul, whom he afterwards appointed his steward. . . . .

"It is quite true that Madame was poisoned, but without Monsieur's knowledge. Whilst these wretches were discussing poor Madame's mode of death, they hesitated as to whether they should inform Monsieur, but the Chevalier de Lorraine said, 'Do not let us tell him; he will never hold his tongue. If he says nothing the first year, he will surely hang us ten years later.' . . . .

"They persuaded Monsieur that the Dutch had given Madame a slow poison, administered in her chocolate. . . . . D'Effiat did not put the poison into the chicory water, but into Madame's own cup. This was intelligently done, for nobody but ourselves drink out of our cup. This cup was not found immediately, but was supposed to be lost, or taken away to be cleaned. One of Madame's servants (who is dead now) told me that very morning whilst Monsieur and Madame were at Mass he had seen d'Effiat come to the sideboard, take up the cup, and rub it with a piece of paper. The servant

* Henrietta of England, Monsieur's first wife.

said to him, 'What are you doing, Monsieur, at our side-board, and why do you touch Madame's own cup?' He answered, 'I am terribly thirsty, and wish to drink. Seeing this cup dirty I began cleaning it with a piece of paper.' That very evening Madame asked for chicory water. The moment that she had drunk it she cried out that she was poisoned. Many present had drunk of this same water, but not out of her cup. . . . . She was immediately put to bed, and, becoming worse and worse, she died two hours after midnight, in the midst of frightful sufferings. . . . ."

"July 21st, 1716.

"Monsieur was very jealous of his children. He used to try and keep them away from me. He allowed me more authority over the Queen of Sicily and my daughter than over my son, but he could not prevent my telling the latter the truth on all occasions. . . . .

"Monsieur did not care for hunting. Indeed, excepting, perhaps, when with the army, he could never make up his mind to ride on horseback. He wrote so badly that he often brought me his letters to read, saying, laughing, 'Madame, you are used to my writing; read this to me so that I may know what I have written.' We often laughed over this together."

"Saint Cloud, Aug. 4th, 1716.

"The King was so attached to all the old customs followed by the House of France that he would never have anything changed in the smallest particular. Madame de Fiennes used to say that Royal families clung so to old traditions that the Queen of England died with a *toquet* on her head; that is a little cap that children wear in bed. . . . .

" When the King desired a thing he never allowed anything to interfere with his wishes. What he had ordered was to be done immediately, and without an observation. He was too much accustomed to say and feel, ' This is our good pleasure,' to suffer anyone to interfere. This made him severe as to the laws of etiquette that he had established. . . . ."

" Saint Cloud, Aug. 12th, 1716.

" The old toad had but little leisure to spend in reading, for she had to read private letters and messages coming from all parts of France, containing special intelligence. Sometimes she received as many as twenty or thirty sheets. She only showed them to the King if it suited her, and according to her love or dislike of certain persons. . . . ."

" Saint Cloud, August 17th, 1716.

" The old wretch is not wanting in cleverness. She speaks with great eloquence occasionally; she could not bear to be styled *Marquise*, preferring by far to be addressed as Mme. de Maintenon. . . . .

" She showed the hatred she bore me in a thousand and one ways; for instance, when the

thwart the King, and finally caused his death by
all the trouble she gave him with the Constitution.
She made my son's marriage, and wished the bastards
to succeed their father; in one word, she ruined
everything. . . . ."

"SAINT CLOUD, Sept. 22nd, 1716.

"I will tell you frankly why I prefer to remain
apart. I am now an old woman and want rest, so I
do not wish to begin what I could never finish. I
never learnt to rule, and know nothing about the
affairs of State, and I am far too old to begin study-
ing such a difficult science. . . . . I have been
much exercised about it, but I remain steadfast.
This kingdom has already been far too much led by
old and young women. It is time for the men to
have a word to say in the matter. I have therefore
made up my mind not to interfere in anything. In
England, the women can govern, but in France if
things are to go well the men must have the command. Where would be the use of my troubling
myself? I only ask for peace and rest. All my
old friends are dead; so why should I fret about
things that do not concern me? My life is all but
ended. I have just the time to prepare myself for
death, and it is difficult to keep a good conscience
in the midst of public affairs."

"SAINT CLOUD, October 29th, 1716.

"We have had few Queens of France really
happy. Marie of Medicis died in exile, the King

was privately married to her first gentleman-in waiting. He treated her very badly. Whilst the poor Queen had neither food nor firewood, he gave great dinners in his own apartment. He was named my Lord Jermyn, Earl of Saint-Albans. He never threw the Queen a kind word. . . . ."

"PARIS, May 14th, 1717.

" Dearest Louise, I have received a visit to-day from a great personage, to wit, my hero, the Czar.* I think him well bred; that is to say, what we used to call well bred: easy in manner, and unaffected in conversation. He is also very witty. Although speaking German in an indifferent manner, he is so intelligent that it is easy to understand his meaning. He is courteous to all, and consequently beloved. I received him in a singular costume. Not being able to wear stays I show myself exactly as I step out of my bed, that is to say, in my nightgown and bed-jacket, and over all a dressing-gown, fastened with a belt."

During the spring and summer of 1717 Madame was so ill that she found it no longer possible to write as long letters as she had been always accustomed to do, and the Raugravine Louise had also an illness about this time, but Madame still wrote to her occasionally, complaining of the frivolity and looseness of the Regent's Court. Although much that went on was necessarily

* Peter the Great.

hidden from her, she heard and saw enough to cause her sincere pain. The conduct of her eldest grand-daughter, the Duchesse de Berri, was far from edifying, and Madame had reason to think that her daughter-in-law was bringing up the Regent's other daughters very badly.

The state of the national finances was getting worse every day. Saint Simon says, " It would take a vast knowledge of finance and a good memory, and the will to write many volumes of matter on the subject, to be able to describe all that was attempted, all that failed, and all that succeeded about this time."

When John Law, a Scottish adventurer, appeared on the scene, the Regent was at his wits' end, and fears were entertained of a national bankruptcy being inevitable. Therefore, when Law propounded his famous scheme of the paper currency, the Regent clutched at the *planche de salut* thus extended to him, eagerly. Law obtained permission to establish a private bank,* the Government promising to accept its bills. But two years later this bank was dissolved and the Royal Bank, with Law as manager, began its career with a great flourish of trumpets.

At this time the interior of North America was all but unknown. The traveller, La Salle, had traversed huge tracts of country which he had appropriated in the name of France, and styled Louisiana, after the King. This country was said

* 1716.

R

to be rich in gold and silver mines and to possess a marvellously rich and productive soil. Law obtained a large grant of land, and started the famous Mississippi, or West India, Company. The shares were taken up wildly as soon as issued, and for a time a flood of commercial prosperity and security set in.

To the Princess of Wales.

"Paris, May 30th, 1717.

"The marriage of the Bavarian Elector to the Princess of Poland clearly proves that no one can escape their destiny, for this is a most unsuitable alliance for that Prince. I hear that he was sent off and married without being told anything about it. His Ministers had been heavily bribed, and they arranged the whole matter so promptly that it was done, so to speak, without his consent being given or asked for."

"Saint Cloud, July 2nd, 1717.

"When Cardinal Mazarin became aware that Monsieur was more advanced in learning than the King, he gave orders to their governor to allow the former to be idle, for he much feared lest he should become more learned than his brother. 'What are you thinking about, M. de la Mothe,' said he to the governor; 'do you intend to make the King's brother into a clever man? If he becomes so mighty learned he will find it hard later on to adopt a habit of implicit obedience ' . . . ."

"Saint Cloud, Sept. 11th, 1717.

"The King had a better opinion of my capacity than I deserved. He was most anxious to appoint me Regent with my son. But thank God that this never came to pass, I should soon have become crazy. . . . . The King often said, 'Madame cannot bear marriages between persons of unequal rank. She finds them absurd,' which was true. . . . ."

"Saint Cloud, Sept. 28th, 1717.

"Whoever bears a personal resemblance to Prince Eugène must be far from handsome. He is even smaller than his eldest brother. All these brothers, with the exception of Prince Eugène, were not worth much. Prince Philip, also a most strange personage, was the second brother. He was fair and very ugly, and died in Paris of smallpox. A third brother, who went by the name of the Chevalier de Savoie, died from a fall off his horse. Prince Eugène was the youngest of them all. He had two sisters, both ugly; one is dead, the other is still in Savoy. . . . . When a young man, Prince Eugène was not very ugly; old age had altered him for the worst. He never looked noble or imposing, but his eyes were not unpleasing."

To the Radgravine Louise.

"Saint Cloud, Sept. 30th, 1717.

"You have doubtless heard that the Pope has caused Lord Peterborough to be arrested at Bologna in Italy. No one here is aware of the reason.

R 2

For four days he walked about dressed in women's clothes. Although clever the poor man is evidently crazy. I hear that he was asked whether he had come to assassinate the Chevalier Saint George by order of the King of England. 'No,' replied he, 'the King would be incapable of ordering such a thing to be done.' He added, 'I could not affirm the same thing of the Prince of Wales.' . . . ."

"Paris, Oct. 22nd, 1717.

" My son is neither handsome nor plain, but he is not unattractive. He is inconstant, never feeling an ardent affection for a long time. On the other hand, his manners are not such as to render him beloved. He is very indiscreet and cannot keep a secret. I have told him hundreds of times how surprised I was that all the women ran after him as they do; they ought rather to fly from him. . ."

"Paris, Oct. 28th, 1717.

" Both in France and England the nobles are excessively haughty, and place themselves above everybody; a little more they would consider themselves superior to the Princes of the Blood, yet many among them are not even noble. I once gave one of our Dukes a good lesson. He was pushing past the Prince de Deux-Ponts to seat himself at the King's table. I observed out loud, 'Why does the Duc de Saint Simon elbow the Prince de Deux-Ponts; is he thinking of taking one of his sons for a page?' Everyone burst out laughing, and so he found himself obliged to leave. . . . .

Lord Peterborough refuses to go out of prison till they have apologised for the affront they made him. If I were in prison and they suddenly offered me liberty I should go off as quickly as possible, and make my remarks from a distance. This lord is an extravagant and curious personage. He would rather die than not say what he thinks of other people, particularly his enemies. I hear that he is in love with the Princess of Wales, and often tells her so, but that he detests the Prince. . . . ."

To the Princess of Wales.

" Paris, Oct. 28th, 1717.

" I only take milk, beer, or wine soup, for I cannot bear broth. . . . . Sausages and ham suit my stomach best. . . . .

"Affection prevented my taking precedence of the late Electress; but with the Duchess of Mecklenbourg and our Duchess of Hanover the case was quite different. Neither would I have passed before Her Highness my mother. I would willingly have even continued carrying her train, but she would not suffer it. . . . . On great occasions Monsieur used to oblige me to put on rouge, greatly to my disgust, for I never cared for dress, and cannot bear anything that puts me out of my usual habits. . . ."

"Saint Cloud, Nov. 5th, 1717.

" The poor Princess (de Conti) was very badly used by her husband. He was jealous as the devil, although there was no sort of reason for it. She never really knew where she would pass the night.

When she was settled in at Versailles he would suddenly take her off to Paris or Chantilly, telling her that she was going to stay there some time, then the next day back they would go to Versailles. She was never at peace for two days together, yet after his death, instead of enjoying the change, she often irritated me extremely by talking of the happy past, and grieving bitterly for the loss of him."

To the Raugravine Louise.

"Saint Cloud, Nov. 13th, 1717.

" I wish that you could learn to play chess. The first Dauphine had a page, aged twelve or thirteen, who knew this game better than the most skilled players. M. le Prince once sent for him, and began a game with him, believing that he would obtain an easy victory. When the boy checkmated him, the Prince went off into such a transport of rage that he tore off his wig, and threw it at the boy's head.

"I am indeed surprised to hear that no account has been printed of the Elector's wedding. . . . . Thank you for the silver medal you sent me; it gave me great pleasure. I have Doctor Luther in gold and silver now. I am convinced that Luther would have done better to reform, and not set up a new religion. He would thus have done a greater amount of good. . . . .

"I assure you that my son has more enemies than friends. His brother-in-law and the latter's wife do everything in their power to injure him with the people. All Mme. de Montespan's children are

wicked reptiles. The little King is a pretty child and very intelligent, but he is spitefully inclined, and cares for no one but his governess. He takes sudden unreasonable dislikes to people, and loves saying painful and unpleasant things. I am not in his good graces, but this troubles me little, for when he attains power, I shall have left this world, and shall no longer be dependent for my comfort on a King's caprice.

"When I warn my son against these wicked people he replies laughingly,* 'You know, Madame, that no one can avoid the fate that God has ordained for him : so if I am destined to die I cannot avoid death, but I will do all that I judge reasonable to ensure my safety, but nothing extraordinary.' My son is very learned. He has a very good memory, and expresses himself well in conversation, but he speaks remarkably well in public. Being but a man he has his faults; but they only injure himself, for he is kindly and good to all those round him."

"Paris, Nov. 29th, 1717.

" I suppose that great rejoicings took place all over England at the safe delivery of the Princess of Wales, but the English are so false that I would not trust them with a single hair. The Duke of

* This is the original text and spelling : " Vous savez bien, madame, qu'on ne peust eviter ce que Dieu vous a de tout temps destines ; ainsi, si je le suis a perir, je ne le pourris eviter ; ainsi je feros que ce qui est raisonnable pour ma conservation, mais rien d'extraordinaire."

Schomberg must be greatly annoyed at only having one daughter, but being still young he may yet have sons, and plenty of them. The Princess of Wales has three sons and three daughters. . . . . I greatly pity the poor Saxons and their Queen. She has, indeed, had a sad existence. I cannot bear the falseness of the King of Poland. He acts without any reference to the solemn engagements he has taken. It is far from Christian to torment people about religion, for when one examines the thing seriously, one sees plainly that religion is made the pretext for ambitious dealings and self-interest. Each serves Mammon and not the Lord. . . . ."

"Paris, Dec. 11th, 1717.

" To trust God implicitly in all circumstances is a great comfort. His wisdom is infinite; He alone knows the reason of all that happens to us. We must submit our wills to His, and as He gave his only Son to ensure us eternal life we ought to feel content and at peace. If He sends us troubles in this life it is to prevent our being chastised for our sins in the next. This ought to afford us great consolation, for it allows us to meet the approach of death without fear. Should He send us happiness, why then let us rejoice and thank Him for His goodness. In this manner God turns all that happens to us to our own advantage as long as we know how to receive His gifts. . . . . Doctor Luther behaved as all the clergy do. They all wish to govern and be the head. Had he thought more of

the general profit of Christianity he would not have made a schism. He and Calvin would have done a thousand times more good had they simply taught, without making such a scandal, and all that was foolish in the Roman religion would have quietly disappeared of itself. . . . ."

"Paris, Dec. 19th, 1717.

" I do all the good that is in my power, as the enclosed * will show you."

"Paris, Dec. 23rd, 1717.

" Lord Stairs has been very ill, but he is now better. His wife excited much admiration by the devoted fashion in which she nursed him, never leaving him day or night. Your praise of her, dear Louise, was indeed merited. I am so troubled about our dear Princess of Wales, that I cried about it yesterday. Her leaving Saint James in the manner described to me by the Countess of Buckenburg is really an unfortunate thing. When her little boys said good-bye to her she fainted from grief. This really moved me."

* This was a letter addressed to Madame by thirty Huguenots, thanking her for interceding for them with the Regent, who caused them to be released from the prison where they had been shut up on account of their faith.

CHAPTER XII.

1718 to 1719.

"Paris, Jan. 6th, 1718.

" Writing does me no harm. Were it otherwise I should long since have died, for I write every day. A great number of letters get lost between England and France. Four of mine to the Princess of Wales never reached her, so you must not be surprised, dear Louise, not to have received the Countess of Buckenburg's epistle. . . . . If our good Germans were rich, they would probably get as luxurious and wicked as are the nations round them. Love of money and self-interest corrupts everybody here. . . ."

"Paris, Feb. 3rd, 1718.

" The last letters I received from England were dated the 16th January, and said that everything was in a sad state. They say here that many are doing their best to set the father and son * against one another, in the hopes that Parliament will appoint a Regent. This is very possible, although it

* George I. and the Prince of Wales.

because the Pope had not allowed his marriage with a near relation of his own."

"Paris, Feb. 29th, 1718.
"8 o'clock in the morning.

"The Princess of Wales assures me that her husband did all that lay in his power to conciliate the King's good graces; that he even begged his pardon, and owned that he had been to blame as humbly as if he had been addressing himself to God Almighty. But the King did not relent. Between ourselves I think that avarice rules all his actions. . . . ."

"Paris, March 6th, 1718.
"8 o'clock in the morning.

"The news sent me from England is no better. The poor Princess is greatly to be pitied. There must be something else at the bottom of all this, where everything is given a double meaning. They say that the King is himself in love with the Princess. I do not believe this, for I consider that the King has in noways a loverlike nature. He only loves himself."

"Paris, March 10th, 1718.

"I see that our Germans are beginning to adopt the English fashion of making away with themselves. This is a fashion that they might quite as well leave alone. . . . The Princess of Wales told me the story of a young man that the King caused to be killed. The lad was only eighteen years of age, yet the King is not in the least

"Paris, March 27th, 1718.

" The Prince of Wales has acted in a noble manner, and if his father does not acknowledge it, nothing will make peace between them. Some people came and begged him to place himself at the head of their party. He replied that nothing would induce him to head a party in the State against the King, his father. You must not be surprised at an Englishwoman behaving rudely to you, for between ourselves that nation is worth very little. The King of England is a bad fellow. He never had any consideration for the mother who loved him so tenderly; yet without her he would never have become King of England. All her children, even the Queen of Prussia, whom she loved so, never treated her as they ought to have done. . . . .

" I am glad that the Princess of Ussingen has got a boy. I hope that the child will resemble his grandfather more than his father. The grandfather was courteous, agreeable, and handsome; the father ugly and foolish. . . . ."

"Paris, March 31st, 1718.

" Historians are greatly given to inventing and lying. I have read in the history of my grandfather, the King of Bohemia,* that the Queen was

* Frederick V., Elector Palatine, married, in 1613, Elizabeth, daughter of James I. He accepted the Crown of Bohemia 1619, lost it 1620, together with the Palatinate. After the Peace of Westphalia his eldest son, Charles Louis, Madame's father, was reinstated in the Palatinate.

"PARIS, April 28th, 1718.

"I received news of the Princess of Wales yesterday. She wrote a most humble epistle to the King of England. He answered with great harshness and made remarks as to her conduct. He will make himself ridiculed by everybody by acting thus, for the Princess has an intact reputation. I cannot understand why the King acts in the manner he does."

"SAINT CLOUD, May 8th, 1718.

" I have to tell you a sad piece of news. I have been crying all the morning for the good and pious Queen of England * who died yesterday morning at St. Germains about seven o'clock. She is assuredly in Heaven, for she gave all she had to the poor. Whole families were kept from starvation by her. She never spoke unkindly of any one, and if one talked to her of others she always said, 'If you know anything against them pray do not tell it to me.' She bore her misfortunes with perfect resignation, and was courteous and agreeable, although she was far from being a beauty. She was always gay, and often praised our Princess of Wales. I had a sincere affection for her, and her death deeply moves me. . . . ."

"SAINT CLOUD, May 29th, 1718.

" Yesterday being my birthday I went to the Carmelite convent to thank the good sisters for the present they had sent me. It consisted of an em-

* Mary of Modena, widow of James II.

"SAINT CLOUD, 19th June, 1718.
"3 o'clock in the afternoon.

"The Queen of England, as far as avarice was concerned, was not in the least Italian, for she never saved a farthing. Indeed she had every royal quality. Her only failing (no one is perfect in this world) was her extreme piety. This was the cause of all her misfortune. She could never save, for she was never regularly paid; on the contrary, she found herself obliged to borrow. It is not true that her servants stole her furniture, for she was lodged in the King's furnished apartments at Saint Germains. . . . .

"There have been but few Queens of England who have led happy lives, neither have the Kings of that country been particularly fortunate. . . . ."

"SAINT CLOUD, June 30th, 1718.
"A quarter-past seven in the morning.

"You ought not to doubt of my affection for you. Are you not the daughter of the father I loved more than my life? It is not your fault that we did not have the same mother. You repair the misfortune of your birth by your many virtues, so how can I help holding you in sincere affection? . . . .

"The King of England will not allow the Prince of Wales to see his children; he has not seen them for six months. I do not think this at all reasonable. Neither has the King allowed the children to visit their mother. The other day the poor little things gathered a basket full of cherries and sent

s 2

it to their father with a message that though they were not allowed to go to him, their hearts, souls, and thoughts were with their dear father always. This brought the tears into my eyes. . . . ."

"SAINT CLOUD, Aug. 4th, 1718.

"Yesterday I received a letter from the Princess of Wales. She said nothing about a conspiration. Talking of conspirations I must tell you that yesterday at the play, my son told me that the Czar had called a council composed of all the bishops and State councillors; then he sent for his son. On the latter's appearing before them the Czar went up and embraced him saying, 'Is it possible that after my having spared thy life thou still meant to assassinate me?' The Prince denied everything. Then the Czar gave the council some papers that had been found in his son's possession and said, 'I cannot be my son's judge. Be merciful to him!' He then retired. The council with one voice condemned the Prince to death. When the Czarewitch was told the sentence he seemed greatly agitated, and remained alone for some hours. Then he asked whether he might see his father once more; this he did in an interview during which he avowed everything, asking his forgiveness with tears. He died repenting of his sins. Between ourselves I believe that they gave him poison to avoid the shame of his being placed in the hands of the public executioner. This is a terrible story and resembles somewhat a tragedy named *Andronic*.

"I thought that M. Law was English, not Scotch. In any case he is extremely unpopular. He seems to me an honest and clever man. . . . .

"People are not kinder here to their children than in England. They put them out to nurse in the country and do not trouble themselves about them for a year or two. I cannot help fancying that many thus become changelings. . . . ."

"SAINT CLOUD, Aug. 25th, 1718.

"Parliament is a source of endless trouble to my son, and excites the populace and citizens of Paris against him more than ever. Every night I thank God that nothing fresh has occurred during the course of the day. Many here would like to have the King of Spain on the throne, for he is feeble and would be more easily led than is my son. Each only thinks of himself. They say that the King of Spain has a right to the throne of France, and that he was unfairly dealt with when sent away from his country. All this is discussed as though the little King's death was a certainty. Should he really die my son would be King, but he would not find himself any surer of his position for that, so the King's death would turn out greatly to his disadvantage. . . . ."

To THE PRINCESS OF WALES.

"PARIS, Oct. 1st, 1718.

"The King * was only superstitious as regarded

* Louis XIV.

religion and miracles. . . . . Unless to those he disliked, he always spoke with great courtesy."

"PARIS, Oct. 16th, 1718.

"The King forgot Mdlle. de la Vallière as completely as though he had never seen her. . . . . She had as many virtues as the Montespan had vices. Her only weakness, her great love for the King, was very excusable; he was young, gallant and handsome. She herself was but a girl, and everyone conspired to ruin her. She was by nature modest and virtuous, and very kind-hearted. I sometimes told her that she had transposed her love, and had given to God all the affection she had once had in her heart for the King.

"Whoever accused La Vallière of loving anyone but the King did her the greatest injustice; but the Montespan cared little how many lies she told to gain her ends."

"PARIS, Oct. 29th, 1718.

"Monsieur was so fond of the sound of bells that he used to come to Paris for All Saints' night on purpose to hear them; yet he did not care for music · · · · He always pretended to be very pious. The soldiers used to say of him, 'He is more afraid of the dust and sun than of being shot,' and this was quite true."

"PARIS, Nov. 1st, 1718.

"My son cannot deny that he is fickle and indiscreet. Once when we saw together a scene in a comedy where a lover tires of his mistress, he

said to me, 'That is exactly the position in which I often find myself.' . . . .

"He has begged my Lord Stanhope to speak to the King of England in favour of your Highness. He says that it is his most earnest wish to see your Highness on good terms with the King, and that he will do his best to bring a reconciliation about, for he feels persuaded that both in your own interest and that of the King's you ought to live together on good terms.

"My son is certainly to be pitied for having such a wife. . . . . He goes to see her every day. If she is in a good temper he stays some time, if otherwise, which is oftener the case with her, he leaves without a word. . . . ."

"PARIS, Nov. 3rd, 1718.

"I feel wretched when I think of all that M. de Louvois burnt in the Palatinate. I expect that he is burning now in the other world, for he died so suddenly that he had no time for repentance. He was poisoned by his doctor, who was in his turn poisoned, but before dying, he (the doctor) acknowledged his crime, but as he was a friend of the old toad's they pretended that he was delirious when he said it. By all this one can see how marvellous is God's justice. We are generally punished by where we have sinned."

Madame was greatly afraid of the Duc du Maine and his treacherous wife, who were always plotting

Maine, was born and brought up in the most evil fashion. His mother was one of the worst women the world has ever seen. I know of three people whom she poisoned, Mdlle. de Fontange* and her child, and a young lady, a friend of the Fontanges. No doubt she poisoned others whose names I do not happen to know. He (the Duc du Maine) was brought up by the Maintenon. That old devil has spent her whole existence struggling to get her pupil placed on the throne, so as to reign with him. She caused him to be legitimised, and would like to see him at the head of the Government, and my son deprived of life and liberty. She had with her our great nobles and the King of Spain. All this causes me to pass many a sleepless night, and his Regency is anything but a happiness to me. . . . I know only too well the wickedness of the old woman. . . . "

"Paris, Nov. 10th, 1718.

"Lord Stairs looks happy and well in health. His wife would like him to be recalled to England. Whilst he remains here she is frightfully jealous, for her husband has a great passion for a pretty woman named Mme. Raymond, who is not only beautiful, but witty, learned, and well-bred. . . . "

"Paris, Nov. 24th, 1718.

"We know now that the rumour of Prince Eugène's death by poison was false news, and as

* A Mistress of Louis XIV.

in Paris they jump from one extreme to the other, there is now a report that he is going to be married. . . . .

"Louvois and such similar wicked people are one mass of vice and falseness. I have often heard that Louvois, the Montespan, and the old woman learnt the art of poisoning from Brinvilliers * herself. Let us hope that it will die with the last of them.† This art is also known at the Court of Berlin, for the Elector and his brother were both poisoned; the youngest died immediately. When they opened him they found in his stomach, diamond powder. . . . ."

To the Princess of Wales.

"Paris, Dec. 5th, 1718.

"The King, Monsieur, the Dauphin, and the Duc de Berri were great eaters. I have often seen the King eat four platefuls of different kinds of soup, a whole pheasant, a plateful of salad, two large slices of ham, mutton with garlic, a plateful of cakes, and then some fruit and hard-boiled eggs. Both the King and Monsieur were very fond of hard-boiled eggs."

"Paris, Dec. 9th, 1718.

"All my life, and from early youth I knew myself to be so ugly that I never took much trouble about dress. Jewels and fine clothes draw attention on those who wear them. It was fortunate that I

* A famous poisoner, Mme. de Brinvilliers.
† Mme. de Maintenon.

Duchesse arrested! They are the heads of the frightful Spanish conspiracy. All has been discovered. Papers were seized at the Spanish Embassy, and those arrested have made complete avowals. The Duchesse, as a Princess of the Blood, was arrested by a Captain of the Guard; her husband, who was in the country, by a lieutenant. The Duchesse was sent to Dijon, her husband to the small castle of Doulens. All the others are in the Bastille. . . . ."

"PARIS, Jan. 7th, 1719.

".The Duc and Duchesse du Maine have written on all sides to try and justify themselves. The thought of their wickedness makes me quite ill. You cannot imagine what infamous libels they have spread about my unfortunate son. . . . .

"All the Duc de Maine's intrigues come from the old Maintenon and the Princesse des Ursins; they are both incarnate fiends. . . . ."

TO THE PRINCESS OF WALES.

"PARIS, Jan. 30th, 1719.

"The Duchess of Zell belongs to a very common family. She would have been lucky had she married one of my gentlemen-in-waiting. . . . ."

"PARIS, Feb. 3rd, 1719.

"There was once an old Princess of Schœningen at Berlin, who was greatly in love with Prince Maurice of Nassau. Being no longer able to walk she had herself carried about in a sedan-chair after

"PARIS, March 5th, 1719.

" It is entirely owing to the Montespan that the
King fell in love with the old toad. Firstly, by
hiding from him the life that had been led by the
creature ; * again she told everyone to praise her
piety, and extol her virtue to the King ; in this
manner he became persuaded that anything said
against her was pure calumny. The Montespan
was very capricious, fond of amusement and hating
to be always alone with the King. Her feeling for
him partook more of the nature of self-interest and
ambition than of affection. To occupy his attention and prevent his seeing what she was about, she
sent for the Maintenon to amuse him. Yet the King,
at first, was not pleased with this arrangement.
He often reproached his mistress with not really
loving him. They constantly quarrelled violently.
This was the Scarron's opportunity. She made
peace between them, and consoled the poor King,
showing him how ill-tempered and disagreeable the
Montespan made herself. This woman had a certain eloquence and fine eyes, so the King grew
used to her and believed that, with her help, he
would soon become a saint. She, whilst making
him understand how greatly she loved him, yet
declared that nothing would induce her to sin or
break God's law. This filled him with admiration
for her, and disgust for the Montespan, who was
always ill-tempered when he came to see her. The

* Dieses Vieh.

taller than her sisters. Saint Beuve says that instead of being called "*Les princesses du sang*," they were nicknamed "*Les poupées du sang*." Madame often refers to her as the "the dwarf," and writes about this time to the Princess of Wales, "The Duc du Maine has just written to his sister (Madame's daughter-in-law), 'Instead of putting me in prison, they ought to have stripped me, and arrayed me in woman's apparel, for having thus allowed myself to be led by my wife.'"

To the Raugravine Louise.
"Paris, March 11th, 1719.

" Here people no longer believe in sorcerers and witches. You would not show yourself our father's daughter if you believed in such things. He was above such superstitions; but when poison or sacrilege is mixed up with these matters, one cannot punish too severely, and I should certainly have such people burnt without mercy. But we ought not to burn witches on the pretext that they fly through the air on broomsticks, or change themselves into cats. If you know any other tales about witches, I should be glad to hear them. . . . ."

"Paris, March 16th, 1719.
" 8 o'clock in the morning.

" At eleven o'clock, I shall go to a Lenten course of sermons that are being given in a church near here. The Abbé does not preach well. He is very different to the Bishop of Clermont, who preaches admirably well. The other says nothing

Although the Regent gave his mother a large present of money in the winter of 1719 rumours of financial difficulty began to be rife. As will be seen in the next letter, Madame complained that everything was getting much more expensive. The offices of the Mississippi Company were situated in the Rue Quincampoix and were already crowded with shareholders eager to turn their paper into gold and silver. The notes began to be looked upon with suspicion by the same people who had realised perhaps only a few weeks before enormous sums by successful speculation with this same paper money, which was at one time actually preferred to specie! It can be easily imagined that Madame did not become aware of what was going on for some time, but she was growing uneasy.

To the Raugravine Louise.

"Paris, March 30th, 1719.

"I cannot believe that the King of England is really going to Hanover; if he does not do so the ladies there will have ordered their fine clothes to no purpose. . . . . I have just received your letter of the 14th. Thank you for the fine ghost stories contained in it. They will give me something to talk about to Mme. d'Orleans, who is, as you may guess, somewhat difficult to entertain.

"Everything here has doubled in price during last year, furniture, clothes, food, and articles of all sorts.

"Every day fresh plots are brought to light.

The Duc de Richelieu goes to the Marquis de Berri, who is faithful to my son, and assures him of his loyalty, asking at the same time for leave to go and join his regiment. Simultaneously, a letter, written by the same Duc to Alberoni, is intercepted, which proves him to have been also mixed up in these plots. My son had him immediately arrested and taken to the Bastille. All the women in Paris are plunged in deep grief, for all the ladies are in love with him. I cannot see the reason of it, for he is an ugly little toad, and far from agreeable in manner. He is also a great coward, impertinent, unfaithful, and indiscreet, yet a certain Royal Princess * is so greatly in love with him that when he became a widower she was determined to marry him, but her grandmother and brother very properly forbade the marriage, for independently of wedding below her rank she would have led a wretched life. . . . ."

"Paris, April 13th, 1719.

"I was truly grieved to hear of the death of your great-niece, but a woman's life is so seldom happy, my dear Louise, that one ought rather to be glad of the death of a little girl-child, for it is a brand saved from the burning. I am more troubled than ever by all that I see and hear round me. I wonder that the fate of Sodom and Gomorrah does not descend from Heaven on France. But these things cannot be written about. . . . . I am concerned to hear that your niece is ill. Could you move her

* Madame's granddaughter, Mdlle. de Valois.

T 2

away from England, and into our good German atmosphere, she would soon recover. The air of London must be making her ill. . . . ."

" Paris, April 14th, 1719.

" La Montespan was fairer than La Vallière; she had a pretty mouth and beautiful teeth, but a bold expression of countenance. One could perceive that she was always intriguing. She had lovely fair hair, and beautiful hands and arms which she did not always keep clean. La Vallière was scrupulously clean.

. " It is owing to the Montespan that the King treated La Vallière so cruelly. Her heart was nearly broken, but the poor creature believed that she would better please God by forcing herself to remain in the Montespan's service. The latter, who was full of spite and wit, publicly mocked at her, obliging the King to treat her in the same manner. His Majesty had a fine spaniel, named Malice. At the instigation of the Montespan he used to pick up the little dog and throw it at the Duchesse de la Vallière, saying, ' Here's your only fit companion,' . . . yet she suffered all this patiently. . . . Her greatest charm lay in her expression of countenance. She had a slight, pretty figure, but ugly teeth; her eyes always seemed to me to be far finer than those of the Montespan. She had a modest demeanour, and was slightly lame, but this did not detract from her charm."

" Paris, April 18th, 1719.

" To-day I must begin my letter in the same strain as Frau von Potíkau of Saxony. When alone in her room, shortly after one of her confinements, she suddenly became aware of the presence of a little old woman dressed in French style. This personage begged her to allow a wedding party to take place in her apartment. Frau von Potikau, having consented to this, some days afterwards there suddenly appeared a large company of dwarfs of both sexes. They brought with them a tiny table, on which were placed a great number of dishes. In the middle of the feast one of their little women ran in saying, ' Thank God, part of our troubles are over; the old beast is dead !' This is what I must announce to your Highness : the old beast is dead ! She died at St. Cyr last Saturday, the 15th of April, between four and five in the afternoon. On hearing of the Duc du Maine's arrest she fainted, and to this may perhaps be attributed her death, for since then she had not had a moment's peace. The anger and disappointment she felt at losing all hope of reigning with the Duc du Maine turned her blood and gave her the measles. For twenty days the fever never left her. A terrible storm then arose and drove in the eruption and finally stifled her. She must have been about eighty-six years of age. I feel sure that the things she most regretted leaving behind her were my son and myself in good health. . . ."

"PARIS, April 22nd, 1719.

"The late King was not so brave as Monsieur, but he was not a coward. . . He was very fond of the Comte de Gramont,* and even allowed him to come to Marly, which was always considered as a great favour. . . . The King often complained of the way in which he had been forbidden to speak to people in his youth, but he was naturally reserved, for Monsieur, who had been brought up in precisely the same way, always managed to gossip with everybody. The King used to say laughing that Monsieur's gossiping ways had disgusted him with the art of conversation. 'Ah!' he would say, 'Must I recount as many foolish things as my brother to please those round me?'"

To THE RAUGRAVINE LOUISE.
"SAINT CLOUD, May 4th, 1719.
"Seven o'clock in the morning.

"I never interfere with Papal matters. I have never had anything to do with the Pope, so you must not address yourself to me for a dispensation.

"It is quite untrue that I changed my name. My only title in France is that of 'Madame,' my husband being the King's brother. Kings' daughters also bear this title, but to distinguish them their christian name is added; thus Henri IV.'s three daughters were known as Madame Elizabeth, afterwards Queen of Spain; Madame Henrietta, after-

* "The Comte de Gramont's Memoirs," by Hamilton, is one of the best known books of the epoch.

wards Queen of England; and Madame Christine, who became Duchess of Savoy. The daughters of the King's brother were known as Mademoiselle, the eldest taking the simple appellation, the other adding some name, thus, Mdlle. de Chartres, Mdlle. de Valois, Mdlle. de Montpensier. The same rule obtains with the King's sons. It is an abuse of style to say the Duc de Burgogne, the Duc de Berri; one ought to say, Monsieur de Burgogne, Monsieur de Berri."

To THE PRINCESS OF WALES.
"SAINT CLOUD, May 10th, 1719.

"The Maintenon was less wicked in the beginning. She grew worse and worse as time went on. It would have sufficed to please me had she died twenty years ago; but for the honour of the late King the event had better have occurred thirty-three years ago, for, to the best of my belief, she married the King two years after the Queen's death, which occurred thirty-five years ago. . . . The great Princesse de Conti was not unfriendly to the Maintenon. . . . It was she who said, when told that she was dying, 'Death will be to me the least of all events.'"

To THE RAUGRAVINE LOUISE.
"SAINT CLOUD, May 13th, 1719.
"Nine o'clock in the morning.

"You asked me to tell you the cause of my late trouble. I cannot tell you all the details, but

moment after the Bishop said to me, 'Could your
Highness make out what the Queen was talking
about? I did not understand a word.' I answered,
'Then why did you answer her?' He replied, 'I
thought I should be wanting in courtesy if I showed
the Queen that I did not understand her.' I began
to laugh so heartily that I had to go away."

"SAINT CLOUD, June 4th, 1719.

"There died in Paris yesterday, at the age
of eighty, a man, who, God forgive him! did
me great harm during my thirty years of married
life. The Marquis d'Effiat, who was Monsieur's
first equerry, and who also held this place
near my son's person. He has left my son a
fine house, but not wishing to accept it my son
is going to return it to d'Effiat's heirs. He
was an extraordinarily rich man. When his
house caught fire, six men could hardly carry the
large cases of gold and silver he had stored up. . . .
It is frightfully hot here. Yesterday a woman
died in a very strange manner. She became so
enormously fat that they feared she had the
dropsy, and gave her remedies suitable for this
complaint, but as she went on swelling they
brought her from Flanders to Paris to consult
Doctor Helvetius, who is a very remarkable physician. He said that he must watch the symptoms
for some days before pronouncing an opinion.
Two days after they found the woman dead in her
bed, stifled by her fat, which had melted from the

great heat. Was not this a strange thing? She
was named Mme. Doujat . . . ."

"SAINT CLOUD, June 6th, 1719.

"The Dauphine was as surely sent into the
next world as if a pistol had been fired at her
head. . . . She often said to me, 'We are both
wretched, but there is this difference between us,
your Highness did your best to avoid coming here,
whilst I did my best to come, so I deserve the
fate that has befallen me.' She cared for the
Dauphin more as a brother than a husband. When
she complained of feeling ill they treated her as
being a crazy woman. A couple of hours before
her death she said to me, 'They will see to-day
that I was not crazy when I complained of feeling
ill.' . . . ."

"SAINT CLOUD, June 14th, 1719.

"La Vallière had not retired from the world
when I first arrived in France; she stayed two
years longer at Court. We became really intimate
together, and her resolution gave me true grief.
I cried bitterly when I saw her charming head hid
under the pall.*

"After the ceremony was over she came to console me, saying that I ought to rejoice with her, for
now began her true happiness. She also thanked
me for my kindness and affection, and said that
she would never forget them.

* One of the ceremonies connected with a Roman Catholic nun's
reception into a religious order.

"SAINT CLOUD, July 17th, 1719.

"The Duchesse de Berri died last night between two and three o'clock in the morning. She died whilst sleeping. My son remained with her till she had lost all consciousness; she was his favourite child . . . ."

"SAINT CLOUD, July 18th, 1719.

"The poor Duchesse de Berri caused her own death as surely as though she had shot herself through the head, for she secretly partook of some melon, figs, and milk. She owned this to me herself. My doctor told me how she had refused to see him or anyone else for fourteen days, during which time she did nothing but eat . . . . As soon as the storm arose she became suddenly worse. Last evening she said to me, 'Ah! Madame, this clap of thunder will greatly injure me.' This was indeed true."

"SAINT CLOUD, July 20th, 1719.

"My son is plunged in such grief that he has lost his sleep. The poor Duchesse de Berri could not have recovered in any case . . . She was buried quietly at night in Saint Denis. Not really knowing how to preach her funeral oration, they made up their minds to do without one.* She declared that she died without regret, having made

* Saint Simon says of this granddaughter of Madame's, "This Princess was a prodigy of wit, pride, ingratitude, evil, obstinacy, and looseness of conduct."

" I made the King laugh heartily by repeating all this to him. . . ."

To the Raugravine Louise.

"Saint Cloud, Aug. 10th, 1719.

" As for the poor Duchesse de Berri's death, I know well to what it is due. That wretched Mouchy killed her as surely as though she had a dagger into her heart. The Duchesse being consumed with slow fever, her favourite brought her all sorts of things during the night, meat patties, melons, salad, milk, prunes, and figs; she also gave her some bad iced beer. For fourteen days she refused to see any doctors, but getting worse and worse had to give way. . . ."

"Paris, Aug. 27th, 1719.

" Mme. de Berri had kept all her husband's fortune, which now came back to the King, as well as her pension. Yet she left many debts. My son will have to pay more than four hundred thousand francs. . . .

" Our dear Princess of Wales is very defective in her spelling, but this is not surprising, for she taught herself to read. I have got used to it now, but at first I found it difficult to understand what she meant. Otherwise she expresses herself in an agreeable style."

To the Countess of Degenfelt.*

Condid Street by Hanover Square, Pony Post, London.

"At Saint Cloud, Friday Sept. 1st, 1719.

" Some time has already past since I received your ladyship's letter of the 20th July; but I found it impossible to reply sooner owing to the great number of letters and visits of condolence that I received. Otherwise I should not have failed to have thanked your ladyship sooner for your kind sympathy during that time you were yourself plunged in affliction. . . .

" Two days ago I received a letter from your ladyship's sister. Are you not afraid of allowing your little daughter to travel so young? The sea must be indeed rough during the month of September.

" I do not write to your ladyship's husband because I understand from the Princess of Wales that he is already on his way here. I should be indeed pleased to see you both, and be able to assure you personally that I am,

" Your Ladyship's very good friend.
" Elizabeth Charlotte."

To the Princess of Wales.

"Saint Cloud, Sept. 8th, 1719.

" The news of the Duchesse de Berri's marriage

* Daughter of Madame's half-sister Caroline, and of the Duke of Schomberg, son of the Marshal of that name killed at the battle of the Boyne.

with that toad* is only too true. He is noble by
birth and allied to several noble families, but even
then he was not worthy of the honour done him,
for he was only a captain in the King's regiment.
All the women ran after him. I think him ugly
and repulsive-looking."

"SAINT CLOUD, September 19th, 1719.
"The late King would willingly have employed
M. Law, but owing to the latter not being
Catholic, the King imagined that we could not
trust him."

"SAINT CLOUD, September 23rd, 1719.
"I have only 456,000 francs,† but if God is
willing I shall not leave this world in debt. My
son has just increased my pension 150,000 francs.
The cause of all the financial difficulties here is the
increase of gambling. I have often been told,
'You do not care for gambling, therefore you are
good for nothing . . . .'"

"SAINT CLOUD, September 29th, 1719.
"A certain person who was, during many years,
constantly near the King's person, and worked with
him every evening in the Maintenon's apartment,
owned to me lately that he had not dared say anything during her lifetime, but that now the old
creature was dead, he could assure me that the late
King had a sincere affection and regard for me, for
he often heard the old witch tormenting the King

* M. de Riom.   † £18,000 a year.

has established his menagery at La Muette. There will be cows, sheep, fowls, goats, and pigeons . . ."

"SAINT CLOUD, October 16th, 1719.

"M. Law is a very clever fellow. He is wonderfully courteous and civil to everybody, and has very good manners. He speaks French much better than most Englishmen do. . . ."

"SAINT CLOUD, October 20th, 1719.

"The Doctor Chirac was called to the bedside of a sick lady. Whilst he was with her some one said that the shares (of Law's bank) were going down. The doctor, who had a great many Mississippis, was much startled, so even when feeling his patient's pulse he muttered to himself, 'going down, down, down!' Hearing this the sick woman began screaming and lamenting, 'Alas!' said she, 'I am surely dying. M. Chirac, when feeling my pulse, whispered 'going down, down, down!' The doctor waking out of his reverie, looked up on hearing this and said, 'You are dreaming, your pulse is regular, and you will soon be quite well. I was thinking of the Mississippi Actions, which are going down in price.' Thus he reassured the sick lady."

Although Madame wrote to the Princess of Wales in September that "The Prince de Conti has at last come to see me, as there happened to be very little doing that day in the Rue Quincampoix, where he generally spends all his time," this very

same Prince de Conti shortly after went to the bank and forced Law to pay him three cartloads of silver in exchange for some of the Mississippi shares, thereby greatly injuring the credit of the Company.

But even at this advanced period the Regent still upheld Law, and issued a degree forbidding the payment of more than one hundred francs at a time in specie, and making the currency of the bank-notes obligatory.

Madame does not seem to have known of this at the time it was done.

To THE PRINCESS OF WALES.

"SAINT CLOUD, Oct. 20th, 1719.

"The Duc de Sully was very absent-minded. Dressing one day before going to chapel he forgot to put on his breeches. It was in winter time, so, going into chapel, he whispered, 'Is it not colder than usual to-day?' Someone answered, 'No, not more than it generally is.' 'Then I must be ill,' said he. 'Perhaps you are lightly clad,' they suggested. This made him lift up his coat and he saw what was missing!"

"SAINT CLOUD, Oct. 22nd, 1719.

"Nobody seems surprised to see me eating black-pudding with pleasure. I have also brought raw ham into fashion. Everyone takes it now; and many of our other German dishes, such as sourcrout, sweetened cabbage, beans and bacon, have been adopted, they are rarely good here. But little game was eaten before I came. I also taught the King to like salted herrings. I have so accustomed myself to German dishes that I cannot bear any French concoction. I only take their roast beef, veal, and sometimes mutton, partridge, or chickens, never pheasants."

"Saint Cloud, Oct. 26th, 1719.

"A Sovereign ought to understand that for him true piety consists in wisely governing his people, and being honourable and just. Whoever tells him otherwise is a bad counsellor. This reminds me of a conversation I once heard at Saint Cloud. A very worthy but severe priest happened to be in Monsieur's apartment. The latter, who dearly liked to play the hypocrite, said, 'I am very thirsty. Would it be breaking the fast to take the juice of an orange?' M. Feuillet,* for so was the abbé named, answered, 'Oh! Monsieur, eat a whole ox, if you like, but be a good Christian and pay your debts!'"

"Saint Cloud, Oct. 28th, 1719.

"Although he is so very clever, I would not be in M. Law's place for all the gold in the world; for they torment him unceasingly, and his enemies spread all sorts of stories and lies about him. . . ."

* The same abbé that attended the First Madame, Henrietta of England, on her deathbed.

"Saint Cloud, Oct. 30th, 1719.

"The Czar is not a madman; on the contrary, he is very intelligent, but it is very unfortunate that he was brought up in so brutal and savage a fashion. I think that the manner in which he has treated the Czarewitch is cruel beyond expression. He gives his son his word of honour that if he comes he will do nothing to him, and when he has come has him poisoned in the Holy Sacrament. This is such an abominable and frightful action that I cannot forgive him. . . ."

"Paris, Nov. 8th, 1719.

"I at first thought well of the Abbé Dubois, because I believed him to be sincerely attached to my son; but when I found out that he was a false beast, only thinking of his own interests and quite forgetting my son's honour and helping him to become as vicious as himself, all my esteem changed into horror. . . . I truly suspected him of having been mixed up in my son's marriage. I know it from my son himself and from friends of the old toad's, to whom Dubois, it seems, used to go by night to betray and sell the secrets of the master who trusted him. . . ."

"Paris, Nov. 21st, 1719.

"I am quite tired of hearing money and shares spoken of round me. . . People come from all the corners of Europe. There are two hundred and fifty thousand people more in Paris than there were a month ago. Stories have had to be added on to houses, and the streets are so full of carriages that many get run over. . . ."

People were beginning to arrive in the hope of converting their paper into gold, but owing to the stringent measure taken by Law and the Regent this was rendered well-nigh impossible. Those who had realised fortunes earlier in the day, having had the sense to reinvest in land or other solid property, could now congratulate themselves upon having made a narrow escape.

Thousands of families who had lived simply, but at their ease, upon a modest competence, were now hopelessly ruined. The following lines, composed about this time, express more eloquently than anything we can say, the past, the present, and the future of Law's great scheme as viewed in 1720 by the Parisians:—

> "Lundi j'achetais des Actions,
> Mardi je gagnais des millions,
> Mercredi je pris équipage,
> Jeudi j'aranjais mon menage,
> Vendredi je m'en vais au bal,
> Et Samedi à l'hôpital."

To the Raugravine Louise.

"Paris, Nov. 30th, 1719.

"I have to announce to you a piece of very good news, namely, the marriage of Mdlle. de Valois to the Prince of Modena. Our envoy started for Rome yesterday to ask for the necessary dispensations, for they are second cousins. The future bride is anything but pleased, for she hoped to wed her

the young page with bitter and scornful words; and he has also retired the permission he had accorded the Prince to see occasionally his little girl. This seems to me cruel and unfair conduct. One would imagine this King to rather belong to the Czar than to the House of Brunswick and the Palatinate."

"PARIS, Dec. 28th, 1719.

"The Prince of Modena is said to be a worthy fellow, intelligent, and pious. He is not handsome, but has been well brought up, and is very reason-able. They say that this Prince fell greatly in love with the portrait of his future wife. I am really sorry for him! Happy couples are things rarely met with. I have seen people who have married for love soon after fall to hating each other like the very devil. Happy are they that are never mar-ried! How contented I should have been had they left me alone, and allowed me to remain single. I will tell you the true reason why Princes and Princesses dislike one another so greatly; it is because they are worth nothing. . . . ."

CHAPTER XIII.

1720 TO 1721.

TO THE PRINCESS OF WALES.

"PARIS, Jan. 9th, 1720.

"I have often walked during night-time in the great gallery of Fontainebleau, said to be haunted by Francis I., but that worthy King never did me the honour of appearing to me. . . . ."

"I was a very lively child. This is why I used to be styled in German *Rauschen petten knecht*. I can remember the King of England's birth as if it had happened yesterday. . . . Whilst playing at hide-and-seek with the little Bulow, I ran into my aunt's room, and hid behind a large screen placed near the door and chimney. When the new-born infant was brought forward I darted out eagerly from my hiding-place to look at it, and was con-demned to a whipping for my curiosity, but in honour of the happy event escaped with a good scolding."

"PARIS, Jan. 24th, 1720.

"M. Law and his children have all become

Catholic, to his wife's great grief. . . . . He is not at all grasping; on the contrary, he distributes much money among the poor, and helps many more privately."

"PARIS, Jan. 25th, 1720.

"The bridal gifts have arrived from Modena, and are composed of a very large jewel that the bride is to wear on her wedding-day, some fine diamonds, and the Duke's portrait. The latter is very ill-painted. All these fine things will only be delivered up after the betrothal has taken place in the King's presence, and the contract has been signed. . . . The Grand Duchess (of Tuscany) says that she is unwilling to receive Mademoiselle,* for she knows Italy well, and believes that Mdlle. de Valois will never become accustomed to their strange ways. She says that she fears, should Mademoiselle take it into her head to return to France, every one would say, 'Here comes the second edition of the Duchesse de Toscane,' or that every time the bride does something foolish, 'Ah! this is owing to the instructions given her by her aunt, the Grand Duchess,' would be instantly said. So she has made up her mind not to speak to her about her future life. . . . ."

"PARIS, Jan. 27th, 1720.

"My son was seeking for the Duchess who is to accompany his daughter to Genoa. Someone who happened to be present, said to him, 'If you

* The bride, Mdlle. de Valois.

"Paris, April 19th, 1720.

"I no longer hold receptions, for it is extremely rare that the Tabouret Court ladies * come to visit me. I had invited them to attend the audience I gave to the Maltese Ambassadors, but not one of them came. During Monsieur's lifetime they eagerly assisted at my receptions, for when a sufficient number were not present Monsieur threatened to inform the King."

"Paris, April 30th, 1720.

"No woman could ever have loved the Duc (de Bourbon). He is very tall, and as thin as a splinter; he walks bent in two, has legs as long as a stork's, a short body, no calves, hollow cheeks, a chin which hardly seems to belong to the face above it, and thick lips; in fact he is very ugly. I have seldom seen such another. . . . ."

On May 21st the Regent issued an edict, which, though meant to restrain, only increased the general state of insecurity and panic, for it reduced both the Mississippi shares and bank notes to one-half of their nominal value. But, owing to the hatred felt by the populace for Law, the Regent, though still his friend, had to withdraw him from his post. Madame writes on the 31st of May, from Paris, to the Raugravine Louise, "My son has been obliged to withdraw Law's place

* So called, because they had the right to sit in presence of Royalty.

have gone better, for I have never given my advice as to anything which touched the Government, neither do I ever meddle in other people's business. But the French are so accustomed to see women take an active part in public affairs that it appears to them impossible that I should remain a stranger to what occurs. These worthy Paris citizens, with whom I am popular, attribute to me all kinds of wisdom. I am very grateful to these poor people for the affection which they feel for me, but I do not deserve it in any way. . . . ."

"Paris, June 14th, 1720.

"Law's good friend, the Duc d'Autin now desires to obtain the latter's late charge for himself. . . . He at first went against Law, but four millions soon brought him to look favourably on his late enemy.

"M. Law is terribly frightened. My son, who is afraid of nothing, notwithstanding the threats constantly addressed to him, makes himself ill with laughing at Law's cowardice. . . . ."

To the Raugravine Louise.

"Paris, June 18th, 1720.

"The Duchess of Hanover need be in no haste to see her new granddaughter, our Mdlle. de Valois, for the latter seems in no hurry to reach Modena. She is very strange, and extraordinarily obstinate. Notwithstanding her father's pressing recommendations, she wishes to visit Provence and go to Tou-

death, and says, ' What is occurring outside, Madame, ought not to be concealed from you. You will find all the Palais Royal gardens filled with the mob, who have brought there the bodies of those trampled to death in front of the Bank.* Law has had to fly. His coach was broken into a thousand pieces and the doors forced open ! ' You may imagine the effect produced on me by this announcement, but I said nothing, for in this sort of crisis it is better to be calm and determined. I went to visit the King as usual, but found such a block in the Rue Saint Honoré that my coach was brought to a stand-still for half an hour. I heard many speak against Law, but nothing was said about my son, and blessings were invoked on my head. At last I arrived at the Palace; there all was quiet, for the mob had retired. My son came to see me. He declared that all the tumult was occasioned by a few drunkards. Those trampled to death had no business to be before the Bank at all, and were in no distress. One of them had a hundred crowns in his pockets, and among those arrested for making a disturbance none were without money. The Palais Royal was broken into by some wretches who hate my poor son. . . . ."

"PARIS, July 21st, 1720.

" Money becomes scarcer every day, but we have plenty of falseness, malice, meanness and ambition

* Three men were trampled to death before the bank during the panic.

to the present Queen of Sardinia and offered to return them to her husband. She answered that the King would be enchanted if I consented to keep them. I had them as a good bargain, for I had bought them by weight, and there were some very rare specimens among them."

"SAINT CLOUD, Aug. 6th, 1720.

"Nobody heard what the King said to the old woman on his death-bed. She went off to Saint Cyr, and though brought back did not even then stay till the end. I feel sure that the King heartily repented of his folly in marrying her. Indeed, notwithstanding all her efforts, he never publicly acknowledged the marriage. Although she wept bitterly when told of the King's death she did not really feel it as she ought to have done. . . . ."

"SAINT CLOUD, Aug. 8th, 1720.

"I can neither speak well or ill of Law's system, for I do not understand it in the least. All that I can see is that it results in all sorts of trouble and annoyance for my son, so I wish that the whole affair had never been heard off. . . . . There is still a great deal of solid money in France, but each hides his through malice, and refuses to put it into business. No one minds M. Law's regulations on this subject.

"None wish for war here. All care above all for luxury, which has never been carried to such a pitch as at the present time. We shall see what all this will result in. . . . ."

"SAINT CLOUD, Aug. 13th, 1720.

"Law is in such a state of terror that he refused to go to Saint Cloud to join my son, although the latter had sent him his own coach. The malice of my son's enemies does not diminish. All kinds of horrible pamphlets are being distributed about him. I cannot understand why he does not severely punish their insolence, but he is the most good-natured of men."

To THE RAUGRAVINE LOUISE.

"PARIS, Aug. 15th, 1720.

"The Parisians are the best people in the world, and if the Parliament was not in existence they would never have risen against lawful authority. The poor people touched me deeply, for they only cried out against Law, not at all against my son; and when I went through the mob in my coach, I heard blessings from all sides. This moved me so much that I could not help crying. It is not at all strange that I am more popular than my son, for his enemies are unceasingly working against him. They make him pass for a tyrant and freethinker, whilst he is the best of men and only too generous.

"I never could understand M. Law's system. I always believed, however, that no good would come of it. I find it difficult to hide my thoughts, so I frankly told my son. He said that I was in error, and tried to explain the thing to me; but the more he explained, the less I could understand anything about it."

x 2

"Paris, Aug. 16th, 1720.

"I think that our Princess of Modena must be very happy if Salvatico is really in love with her, for as he is in constant communication with people here, he is able to inform her of all that goes on in her native country. . . . ."

"Salvatico is one of the greatest fools in existence. He is a great favourite of the Duke of Modena, which shows the truth of the old German proverb: 'like flies to like, said the Devil to the chimney sweep.'

"Saint Cloud, Aug. 18th, 1720.

"All is still calm here, but M. Law no longer dares go out. The Women of the Halles * have placed little boys round his house as spies, to be told the moment he leaves. This is a bad look-out for him, and I fear some fresh rising."

"Saint Cloud, Aug. 21st, 1720.

"I have never yet met a Scotchman or an Englishman so cowardly as is M. Law. Fortune destroys courage. One does not easily abandon what one possesses of the goods of this world. I think that there are moments when he must wish to find himself at the Mississippi or in Louisiana.

"It thunders daily, but no real harm is done to man or beast; yet curious things happen. It took every hair off a man's body without hurting him. It broke the belt of a sword which an officer had

---

* A corporation of Paris market-women.

she lost consciousness, and had to be carried away
from the garden. . . . ."

" Saint Cloud, Sept. 6th, 1720.

"I have received during the last few days several
anonymous letters threatening to burn me here, and
my son at the Palais Royal. My son never speaks
or tells me a word of what is going on round us.
In this he follows the example of his father, who
used to say, 'All is well as long as Madame does
not know it.'"

" Paris, Sept. 20th, 1720.

"Three days ago I received another anonymous
letter, the contents of which caused me much merri-
ment. It counselled me to cause my son to be shut
up as being a lunatic, and assured me that that was
the only way to save his life. . . . .

"My son has already slept several times at the
Tuileries; but I fear that the King will never become accustomed to his presence, for my son has
never known how to win children; he does not like
them."

To the Raugravine Louise.

" Paris, Oct. 3rd, 1720.

"The irregularity of the post, my dear Louise,
is due to M. de Torcy's dislike of me and to the
Archbishop of Cambrai's curiosity. The latter
wishes to know all I write, and as they cannot make
my son quarrel with me they try to set others
against me. They told the Maréchal de Villeroi
that I had written to my daughter that he and all

those said to belong to the old Court were my son's enemies. I answered coldly, ' It is true that I wrote thus to my daughter, and I wrote the truth, for the ambassador of Spain's letters alone prove it."

To the Princess of Wales.

"Paris, Oct. 4th, 1720.

"My son was much beloved, but since the advent of that accursed Law, he has been hated. Hardly a week passes but I receive by post letters filled with terrible threats, and where my son is spoken of as the greatest monster and tyrant. . . . .

"A certain preacher said in one of his sermons that the Last Judgment would take place in the Valley of Josaphat. Someone thereupon tried to prove to him that there would not be enough room. He answered, ' Not at all; those who cannot enter will remain outside.' "

"Paris, Nov. 9th, 1720.

" The Mississippi is the cause of as many troubles in Paris as is the South Sea in London. Last week a man jumped from a window and broke his neck. I would not be in Law's skin for worlds. He has too much to answer for before God. If the French take it into their heads to imitate the English fashion of destroying oneself, as many will perish as during the Plague, for everything quickly spreads in this country. The Baron Gory wrote me lately that the Kings of England and Prussia had made up their minds to interfere on behalf of the inhabitants of the Palatinate. A Sovereign ought not

to dislike his subjects. He ought on the contrary to care for them as a father, otherwise he must account for it before God.

" I have seen a Genoese prophecy, saying that in the year 1727 the world will be entirely destroyed and burnt up to such an extent that it will become a globe of glass.

" I forget if I sent you a certain song about the Archbishop of Cambrai.* I can sincerely assure you that I do not know a greater rogue, nor one more false. What troubles me exceedingly is, that my son, who knows him as well as I do, only listens to and favours this little devil."

Madame's intense dislike to the Abbé Dubois was well known to everybody in the Regent's Court, and Saint Simon says that on being first informed of her son's Regency, "Madame, overjoyed, embraced the Regent warmly, and said that she had but one thing to ask of him, namely, to give up having anything to do with the Abbé Dubois, who was the greatest rogue and rascal on the face of this earth."

On his appointment to the Archbishopric of Cambrai these verses were sung all over Paris:

" Je suis du bois dont on fait les cuistres,
Et cuistre je fus autrefois,
Mais à présent je suis du bois
Dont on fait les Ministres."

---

* The infamous Abbé Dubois, who is now known to have exercised an evil influence on both the public and private life of the Regent.

His influence over the Regent was unbounded. This was probably owing to the fact that he had at one time been his tutor.

To the Princess of Wales.

"November 20th, 1720.

"The Princesse de Siegen must surely be more agreeable in manner than is her husband, a sadly tiresome personage, whom, the Lord be praised, I have not seen for a long time. He once came and told me that I ought to support and uphold him to the best of my power. I asked him the reason. He replied that it was because he was a Roman Catholic, and therefore preferable to all the other Princes of the House of Nassau, who were Huguenots. I began laughing, and assured him his religion was his own business, not mine; also that I had always greatly esteemed the House of Nassau, and that I thought equally well of all of them, whatever might be their religions. He became as red as fire and withdrew, much ashamed. . . . ."

"Paris, Nov. 28rd, 1720.

"My aunt, our dear Electress, being once at the Hague, did not visit the Princess Royal,* but the Queen of Bohemia † did so, and took me with her. Before starting my aunt said to me, 'Lisette, do not behave in your usual flighty manner. Follow

---

* Mary Henrietta, daughter of Charles I., married, in 1650, to William of Nassau, Prince of Orange.
† Elizabeth Stuart, daughter of James I.

"PARIS, Dec. 24th, 1720.

"M. Law is in Brussels. Mme. de Prie lent him her post-chaise. When sending it back he wrote to thank her, and sent her a ring worth a hundred thousand francs. The Duke provided the relays and sent four of his own servants with him all the way. . . . ."

"PARIS, December 27th, 1720.

"When saying goodbye to my son, Law said to him, 'I have committed great faults, Monseigneur, but you will neither find malice nor dishonesty in my conduct.' His wife refuses to leave Paris till all their debts are paid. They owe ten thousand francs to their cook alone *. . . . ."

"PARIS, Dec. 28th, 1720.

"The Princesses are so badly brought up in this country that it has become a public scandal. A little care would make it all otherwise, for my daughters, whom I brought up carefully, are as different as possible. No princesses in Europe get on better with their husbands than the Queen of Sardinia † and the Duchess of Lorraine.‡ But when children are allowed to have their own way from seven to twenty, nothing but ill can result from it. As for myself, I have done my duty; I will no longer

---

* Law retired to Venice, where he died in 1729.
† Madame's step-daughter, daughter of Henrietta Maria of England.
‡ Madame's own and only daughter, married to the Duke of Lorraine.

Duc de Noailles, who glared angrily at the former. I did not then know the reason of these angry looks, but yesterday I learnt all about it. Two years ago Prince Charles married the Duc de Noailles' daughter. . . . She is a very virtuous and sweet woman, and much attached to her husband, who is a remarkably handsome man . . . yet he affected complete indifference to her, although she is both pretty and well-behaved. The day before yesterday morning, Prince Charles went to her and said quietly, 'Madame, the time has come when we must separate, for I can no longer afford to keep you.' The poor little wife, much frightened, replied, 'Is there anything in my conduct which displeases you? If there is, pray tell me, and I will try and amend my manners. As for the expense of my keep, I will consent to live in a garret, and on bread and water, rather than separate from you. To this he observed, 'I am quite satisfied with your conduct, and have nothing to complain of in your manners, but I may as well tell you once for all that you inspire me with aversion. I detest the sight of you, so you must resign yourself to going back to your father.' She then began weeping bitterly, but he only said, 'What is the use of shedding these tears, they do not move me in the least, so do go away.' 'Nay,' said she, 'if it be indeed as you say, I cannot go back to my father's house, but must go and hide my shame in some secret place.' Thereupon she sent for all her

grieved to lose me. His visits do me far more
good than does the physic I am ordered to take,
for they rejoice my heart and do not give me
pains in my stomach, and he always tells me something funny, which makes me laugh. He is so witty
and agreeable. I should be indeed an unnatural
mother did I not love him with my whole heart.
If you knew him you would see how entirely
free he is from malice and ambition. Ah! he is
only too good! He forgives everybody and does
nothing but laugh at his enemies. If he made himself more feared by his wicked relations, they
would hesitate before beginning their machinations
against him. You cannot figure to yourself the spite
and personal ambition of our Princes. . . . ."

"PARIS, April 12th, 1721.

"We have just been informed of the death of
the Queen of Denmark. I shall go into mourning
to-morrow, but only wear it a month. They say
that the King of Denmark was much troubled, and
fainted after the Queen had bidden him adieu. This
grief comes rather late in the day. Perhaps the
poor Queen had no reason to be so jealous of her
husband. In her place I should have been only too
glad to have occasionally got rid of him; he was so
ugly and stupid. I think that I see him now
dancing at Versailles with my daughter. He hardly
seemed to know what he was doing, and kept opening his mouth and staring round him. The King
said to me, 'Do go to your poor nephew's assist-

"The cabbages are not good either, owing to the earth being sandy and poor in substance. Ah! how glad I should be to partake of some of the dishes your cook makes for you! They would be more to my taste than all the fine things concocted by my *maître d'hôtel.* . . . ."

The following * dinner ordered and eaten by Madame, and the prices she paid for everything of which it was composed may interest the reader—

Dinner.

"Soup, composed of chicken-broth and veal, 10 livres, 9 sols" (about eight shillings).

"Two boiled chickens, served in vermicelli, 22 sols" (about one shilling).

"Duck and cabbage, 44 sols" (about one shilling and tenpence).

Even making due allowance for the difference in the value of money, Versailles prices must have altered considerably since the days when the King's sister-in-law could procure a good dinner for about eleven shillings, comprising three chickens and a duck.

Although Madame never saw her prophesy fulfilled, she foresaw the ignominious retreat in 1734, to France, of her third granddaughter, Mdlle. de Valois, whose marriage to the hereditary Prince of Modena had caused so much rejoicing in the Regent's family in 1720.

* Taken from a curious work by Monteil, *Matériaux Inédits pour l'Histoire.*

have married him, for he was small and ugly. . . .
I was then quite of age to be married, for the Duke
has been dead forty-three years. God alone knows
when I shall follow him ; but as long as the Lord
watches over my children I feel at peace. . . . ."

" The late Princesse d'Epinoy was a strange
woman. One night a robber found his way into
her apartment, and threatened to stab her with a
dagger if she did not immediately give him up all
her money. She did not hesitate a moment, but
flew boldly at him, and seizing his neckcloth
nearly strangled him, screaming to her servants
meanwhile. When they arrived she ordered the
robber to be taken to the stables. ' Only spare my
life ! ' cried he ; so she had him severely beaten
and then sent on his way. . . . ."

" Paris, July 19th, 1721.
" There is a vast difference between being really
a native of a country and only learning the
language there roughly through having arrived
when one was already grown up. If your niece,
the Countess von Degenfelt, loves her husband, she
will be pleased with everything round her, for true
love is a sauce which suits every dish, as says the
prologue in *Pourceaugnac,**

'Quand deux cœurs s'aiment bien
Tout le reste n'est rien.'

_____

* One of Molière's comedies.

three o'clock, namely, the reception of that wretch, Cardinal Dubois . . . . I shall be obliged to salute him and mutter a few gracious words. This will go much against me, but now pain and vexation compose the chief of my diet. But I see the Cardinal arriving and must make off. The Cardinal begged me to forget the past, and made me the finest speech in the world. His cleverness cannot be denied, and were he as honest as he is intelligent there would be nothing left to wish for in that direction."

The next event in Madame's life was the betrothal of her granddaughter, Elizabeth Louise, fourth daughter of the Regent, officially styled Mdlle. de Montpensier, to the Prince of Asturias, eldest son of the King of Spain.

This Princess was married on the 20th of January of the following year, and became Queen of Spain in 1724, but, being widowed within the same year, she returned to France and died in the Palace of the Luxembourg in 1742.

Madame shows her pleasure in this marriage in a few words addressed to her half-sister on the 2nd of Oct., 1721:

"I can only write you a few lines this morning, my dear Louise, for I am hastening to Paris to congratulate my son and his wife on the good news I have just been told. The King of Spain has sent to ask them for the hand of their daughter for his eldest son, the Prince of Asturias. Mdlle.

unaccompanied, and mixing in church with all the
common people. The Maintenon had forbidden
everybody to inform the King of all this, for
fear that if he reproved the Dauphine, she would
become sulky, and no longer serve to enliven His
Majesty . . . . ."

TO THE RAUGRAVINE LOUISE.

"PARIS, Oct. 23rd, 1721.

"I send you the letter * I promised, from the
King of Bohemia † to his wife. ‡ It is a curious
missive:—

'STRABACH, this 21st—31st of March, 1652.

'MY DEAREST HEART,

'I received your dear letter of the 4th–14th
March; since then I have not been able to write
to you. What troubles me not a little is that our
letters are so often intercepted. This prevents my
writing anything that all may not read . . . . .

'This morning I went to Nuremburg. I never
saw a finer town nor one more peopled. . . . .

'I fear that our affairs in the Palatinate are not
going on well. The Duke of Holstein informs me
that the jewels and money belonging to our late
grandmother are to be divided into five portions,
and that your mother's share will be given to the
King of England. This would be most unfair. . . .

* Written in French.
† Frederick V., Elector Palatine, Madame's grandfather.
‡ Elizabeth, daughter of James I.

'As for my own affairs, I do not know what to
say of them. I hope to God that all will go well,
and that I shall soon have the happiness of seeing
you and assuring you that I am, my precious heart,
your very faithful friend and affectionate servant,

'FREDERIC.'

"The citizens of Nuremburg have presented the
King with two groups, forming the terrestial and
celestial globes, strangely fashioned."

Describing Mdlle. de Montpensier just after her
departure for the frontier of Spain, Madame says
to the Raugravine, "I do not think that Mdlle. de
Montpensier can be considered an ugly girl, for she
has fine eyes, white smooth skin, a pretty nose, and
a very small mouth. But she is the most unpleasant
creature I ever saw in my life. The manner in
which she speaks, eats, and drinks, gets on my
nerves, and she did not shed a single tear in quitting
us here. I have witnessed two of my relatives, and
now my granddaughter, become Queens of Spain.
Of these my favourite was my stepdaughter, whom
I loved dearly, for when I first arrived in France
she was my closest friend, being only nine years
younger than myself. I remember that we were
all so childishly inclined that we used to play
games with Charles Louis and the young Prince
d'Eisenach. . . . ."

"PARIS, Nov. 22nd, 1721.

"What you say as to these times and my present

position, shows me how little you understand this Court and people. Would to God that the late King were still here! During his lifetime I had more to pleasure me in the course of one day than I have had during the six years of my son's Regency. Then, there was really a Court. We did not lead this *bourgeois* existence. I, who have been accustomed to a Court all my life, cannot get used to this state of things. Once I had my son with me whenever I wanted him ; now I hardly ever see him. Even in Paris, where we share the same antechamber, I often do not perceive him for three whole days. His Regency causes me untold anguish, for I am always thinking that he will be brought in assassinated by one of his infamous enemies. . . . ."

"Paris, Feb. 21st, 1722.

" Large, stout strong people live less long than small, mean personages. This has been clearly proved by the poor Princesse de Ratgotzé. Last Sunday she was strong and hearty ; Monday saw her dead ! They buried her yesterday in her own convent. Her people tell a most extraordinary tale about her. It seems that when at Varsovia she dreamt one night that she found herself in an unknown chamber with a stranger, who offered her a cup and bade her drink. Not being at all thirsty she refused ; but he insisted, saying that it would be the last time she would partake of anything in this life ; then she awoke. She never forgot this strange

dream. On arriving here she lodged in an inn. Feeling ill she sent for a doctor, and they brought Helvetius, one of the King's physicians. He is a clever man, much thought of by all. His father was a Dutchman. On seeing him enter, the Princess became greatly agitated, and on Count Schlieben asking her what was the matter, replied that Doctor Helvetius exactly resembled a certain man whom she had seen in a dream at Varsovia. Then laughing, she added, ' But I shall not die here, for this is not the apartment which I saw at Varsovia.'

" When she moved into the convent at Chaillot and saw the chamber she was destined to occupy, she said to her people, ' I shall not leave this place as a living woman, for this is the apartment I saw in my dream, and where I shall drink for the last time in life.'

" And so it happened. It seems to me that these adventures happen more to those belonging to the Hesse branch of the family than to any one else, God alone knows only. We, of the Palatinate, see neither spirits or visions . . . . ."

To the Princess of Wales.
"Paris, March 10th, 1722.

" Prince Emanuel of Portugal's story reminds one of a romance. They say that at first his mother intended him to become priest and bishop, but that the Prince refused. They say that he was greatly in love in his own country. The King sent for him and asked him if it was indeed true that he refused to take orders. The Prince answering that it was so, the King, I hear, gave him a box on the ear, to which the infant answered, ' You are my King and my brother, so I cannot revenge myself for the insult you have just given me, but I shall go away and you will never see me again,' and he left that same night. The King had ordered him to go from Paris to Holland, but little heed gave he to that. Neither the Ambassador here nor his Governor knew of all this, so when the Prince announced to them that he was desirous of seeing Marly and Versailles, the Ambassador and the governor did all to pleasure him, and went with him to Versailles. On their return from their expedition the Prince suddenly asked, ' Is there not a post-chaise here ? ' ' Yes,' they answered, ' there are even four of them, your Highness.' Turning to the astonished Ambassador he said graciously, ' I wait for an opportunity of proving to you my friendship and gratitude. I am just going to start for Vienna, where, no doubt, the Emperor, my cousin, will receive me suitably. I will learn the art of war, fighting against the Turks with his army.' He then thanked his governor for all his care of him, and added that were he ever happy the other should share in his good fortune were God willing. He also spoke to all the gentlemen. After this he entered into one of the post-chaises and went off . . . . .

" ' Oh ! ' said the King, much relieved, ' if that is all, take him and welcome.' "

To the Raugravine Louise.

" Paris, May 16th, 1722.

" I am, indeed, grateful to you for your prayers, though I do not desire happiness in this world as long as God protects my children; but pray that my life beyond the grave may be a happy one, and also intercede for my son. The only grace I ask of God is his conversion. I do not believe that there are a hundred Christians in Paris at the present moment, even amongst the clergy. This state of things makes one shudder . . . . . "

To the Princess of Wales.

" Paris, May 21st, 1722.

" After Monsieur's death the King asked me where I wished to go—to a Paris convent or to Maubuisson. I answered that, as I had the honour to belong to the Royal household, I should naturally accompany it everywhere, and should begin by going to Versailles with everyone else. The King seemed pleased at my decision, though he observed that he had asked me the question because he had reason to think that I did not care to be with him. I replied that I could not imagine who could have told His Majesty anything so false about me, and that I had certainly more affection for him than those who had thus borne false witness against me. Thereupon the King sent everyone away, and spoke with great frankness,

accusing me of hating Mme. de Maintenon. I owned that this was true, but ascribed my hatred of her to my knowledge of the ill she worked me with His Majesty. But I added, that to pleasure him I would consent to receive her, and become reconciliated with her. The good woman had never thought that I should act with such wisdom, or she would never have allowed the King to come near me. He sent for her, and said, ' Madame has consented to receive you.' He made us embrace one another, and so ended the affair. But she continued injuring me in every way in her power. . . . . As for a convent, that would not have suited me at all; but it was just what the old woman hoped to oblige me to do. Montargis is my dower-house, but is worth nothing. I live on the King's bounty. They began by giving me nothing at all after my husband's death. . . . . What would have been my fate had I chosen to retire to Montargis ? "

" Saint Cloud, June 15th, 1722.

" The Dauphin * was very intelligent, and truly pious; but he had one defect, that of allowing his wife to manage him as though he was a child. She could make him believe anything she liked. He certainly proved his love for her by dying of grief eight days after her death. He always said that it would be so. A famous Turin astrologer once told

* The Duc de Bourgoyne.

the Dauphine her fortune. He predicted all that
would happen to her till her twenty-seventh year,
when her career would be cut short by death.
She often spoke of this, for all that he had foretold
really happened to her year by year. One day
she said to her husband, 'The hour of my death
must now be approaching; you cannot remain a
widower, on account of your rank and piety; pray
tell me the Princess you mean to choose?' He
answered, 'I hope that God will never inflict on
me the pain of seeing you depart this life; but
should this misfortune befall me, rest assured that
I shall never marry again, for I shall follow you in
eight days to the grave.' And so it exactly happened. Eight days after the death of his wife he
also died. This is a true story, not a romance.
Often, though fresh and hearty, the Dauphine
would say, 'I must make haste to enjoy my life,
for I shall die this year.' I used to think that she
said it as a joke, but it was only too true. The
moment she fell ill she declared that she knew
death was approaching."

"Saint Cloud, July 2nd, 1722.

"The Queen-Mother* could feel at rest, àpropos
of Cardinal Mazarin. As he was not an ordained
priest he was free to wed her. The whole of this
affair is now known to us all. I have often seen
the secret passage through which they communicated
with each other when at the Palais Royal. . . . ."

* Anne of Austria.

Preparations were being made for the solemn
coronation of Louis XV. at Rheims, and Madame
was long in making up her mind to take so long a
journey in her weak state of health. In September
she writes to Herr von Harling, "I follow out my
physician's orders to avoid being spoken to by my
son about it; but all must be as God wills it to be,
and I feel quite resigned." And two days later,
having been informed that her daughter, the
Duchesse de Lorraine, was going to Rheims with
her children, she writes again to Herr von Harling,
"I am in exactly the same state as when I last
wrote to you; the future is in God's hands. I am
getting ready for my journey to Rheims. Time
will show whether the result will be good or evil.
I sent you your nephew's letter, and I can assure
you that whatever happens I will remain your true
and faithful friend."

To the Raugravine Louise.

"Paris, Nov. 8th, 1722.

"I arrived home * the day before yesterday, but
in a sad state During my journey I received five
of your dear letters, and I thank you for them most
sincerely; they afforded me great pleasure. I did
not answer you whilst away, both owing to my
general weakness and the want of time, for I had
my children constantly with me, and visits from
many distinguished people, including Princes,
Dukes, Cardinals, Archbishops, and Bishops who

* At the Palais Royal.
z

came to see me. I do not think it would be possible to conceive a more beautiful sight than the King's coronation. If God gives me time I will give you a description of it. My daughter was much moved on seeing me. She had never really believed in my illness, thinking that I was only fatigued with all I had gone through in the last few years. But when she saw me at Rheims she was so shocked by my appearance that the tears came into her eyes. Her look quite troubled me. Her children are much grown and fine looking. . . . . I should like to talk to you thus a little longer, but I feel too tired to do so. . . . ."

"Paris, Nov. 12th, 1722.

" I hope to be able to send you an account of the coronation the day after to-morrow. I know of nothing fresh to tell you to-day, excepting that I have been informed of something which causes me great joy, namely, that my son has definitively dismissed all his mistresses and former boon companions, and that, were it only for the young King's sake, he will find it impossible to continue his old way of life. I hope that God will assist him in remaining firm to these good resolutions. It is the only matter that troubles me; for the rest, let God dispose of me as He will. . . . ."

"Paris, November 21st, 1722.

"I get worse every hour and suffer incessant pain, from which nothing relieves me. I greatly need that God shall inspire me with patience. Do not grieve should you happen to lose me, for it would be for me a great happiness to be delivered from my sufferings . . . . ."

"Paris, November 29th, 1722.

" You will only receive a very short letter to-day. I am worse than ever, and cannot sleep. Yesterday morning we lost our poor Maréchale.* She died quietly, without any special disease having attacked her. Her death has really grieved me, for she was a worthy and clever woman. No one can be surprised at the death of a person of eighty-one years of age, yet it is painful to lose a friend whom one has known fifty-one years. But I must leave off now, dear Louise. I am in too great pain to be able to add another word. If you saw the sad state I am in, you would understand my longing for the end . . . . ."

Madame died nine days after this letter was written, in the Regent's arms, but far from her daughter, who did not hear of her mother's death till some days later.

Marais wrote in his diary five days before her death, " Madame is very ill, and all hopes have been abandoned. Physicians are arriving from all sides and promise to surely cure her, but she only says that they are all quacks, and that she is content to die. (This was very characteristic.)

---

* The Maréchale de Clérembant.

She is very courageous and steadfast, and did not mind the journey to Rheims, saying that death is the same wherever you happen to meet him. She said to her son, ' Why do you weep ? Must we not all end by dying in this world ?' and to a lady who wished to kiss her hand, ' You can embrace me if you like, for I am going to a land where all shall be equal in the sight of God.' We are about to lose a good Princess ; a rare and precious thing in these times . . . . ."

She was interred in Saint Denis, and Masillion preached her funeral oration.

Writing on the 15th of December to the Marquise d'Aulade, the Duchesse de Lorraine says : " I am so overwhelmed with grief that it is impossible to write at length. I may truly say, in Madame's loss I lose all, and death will be welcomed by me now, as a means to rejoining her." To Madame, notwithstanding Saint Simon's implication that Mademoiselle de Chartres had been glad to leave her mother when she married the Duc de Lorraine, she bore a true and vivid affection.

In a quaint inventory, drawn up immediately after Madame's death, of the furniture in her apartments we find :

One long bed, nine feet square, English tapestries comprised of grotesque subjects.

French ditto, recounting Ovid's *Metamorphoses*.

One white satin carpet.

In her boudoir, three chairs, tapestries.

Fifty pieces of rare porcelain and a great many looking glasses, besides a strange collection of curios.

One detail connected with her death would have sorely vexed her. Cardinal Dubois bought up all the black materials very cheaply and sold them at a large profit, on Madame's death being officially notified to the good people with whom she had always been so popular, notwithstanding her son, the Regent's, many private sins, and his connection with the too famous Mississippi Company.

THE END.

WESTMINSTER : PRINTED BY NICHOLS AND SONS, 25, PARLIAMENT STREET.

New Publications.

The POLITICAL LIFE OF OUR TIME. By
DAVID NICOL. 2 vols. demy 8vo.

REMINISCENCES of a REGICIDE.   Edited
from the original MSS. of Serjeant Marceau, Member of the Convention,
and Administrator of Police in the French Revolution of 1789.   By
M. C. SIMPSON.   Demy 8vo. with Illustrations and Portraits.

HALF-A-CENTURY of MUSIC in ENGLAND:
1837-1887.   By F. HUEFFER, Author of "Richard Wagner and the
Music of the Future."   Demy 8vo. 8s.

FROM PEKIN to CALAIS by LAND.   By
H. DE WINDT.   With numerous Illustrations by C. E. Fripp, from
Sketches by the Author.   Demy 8vo. 20s.

TEN YEARS' WILD SPORTS in FOREIGN
LANDS; or, Travels in the Eighties. By H. W. SETON-KARR, F.R.G.S.,
&c.   Demy 8vo. 9s

HISTORY of the PEOPLE of ISRAEL.
FIRST DIVISION : TILL THE TIME OF KING DAVID.
SECOND DIVISION : FROM THE REIGN OF DAVID UP TO THE CAP-
TURE OF SAMARIA.
By ERNEST RENAN.   Demy 8vo. 14s.

MADAME DE STAËL : her Friends and her
Influence in Politics and Literature.   By Lady BLENNERHASSETT.
Translated from the German by J. GORDON CUMMING.   With a
Portrait, 3 vols. demy 8vo, 36s.

NEW BOOKS FOR APRIL.

TEN YEARS' WILD SPORTS IN FOREIGN LANDS;
Or, Travels in the Eighties. By H. W. SETON-KARR, F.R.G.S., etc. Demy 8vo.

MADAME DE STAËL: Her Friends, and Her Influence
in Politics and Literature. By LADY BLENNERHASSETT. With a Portrait. 3 vols.
Demy 8vo, 36s.

HISTORY OF THE PEOPLE OF ISRAEL. From
the Reign of David up to the Capture of Samaria. By ERNEST RENAN. Second
Division. Demy 8vo, 14s.

FROM PEKIN TO CALAIS BY LAND. By H. DE WINDT.
With numerous Illustrations by C. E. FRIPP from Sketches by the Author. Demy 8vo,
20s.

THE HISTORY OF ANCIENT CIVILISATION.
Handbook based upon M. Gustave Ducoudray's "Histoire Sommaire de la Civilisation."
Edited by REV. J. VERSCHOYLE, M.A. With Illustrations. Large crown 8vo, 6s.

HALF A CENTURY OF MUSIC IN ENGLAND.
1837—1887. By F. HUEFFER, Author of "Richard Wagner and the Music of the
Future." Demy 8vo.

THE MARRIAGES OF THE BOURBONS. By CAPT.
THE HON. D. A. BINGHAM. 2 vols. Demy 8vo.

GALILEO AND HIS JUDGES. By F. R. WEGG-PROSSER.
Demy 8vo, 5s.

THE LIFE OF THE RIGHT HON. W. E. FORSTER.
By T. WEMYSS REID. Fifth Edition. In 2 vol. Demy 8vo, 10s. 6d.

GIBRALTAR. By HENRY M. FIELD. With numerous Illustrations
Demy 8vo.

THE SALMON AND ITS HABITS. By MAJOR TRAHERNE.
Crown 8vo.

A SUBURB OF YEDO. By T. A. P. With Illustrations.
Crown 8vo.

BARTLEY (G. C. T.)—
A HANDY BOOK FOR GUARDIANS OF THE POOR.
Crown 8vo, cloth, 3s.

BAYARD: HISTORY OF THE GOOD CHEVALIER,
SANS PEUR ET SANS REPROCHE. Compiled by the LOYAL SERVITEUR.
With over 200 Illustrations. Royal 8vo, 21s.

BEATTY-KINGSTON (W.)—
A WANDERER'S NOTES. 2 vols. Demy 8vo, 24s.
MONARCHS I HAVE MET. 2 vols. Demy 8vo, 24s.
MUSIC AND MANNERS: Personal Reminiscences and
Sketches of Character. 2 vols. Demy 8vo, 30s.

BELL (JAMES, Ph.D., &c.), Principal of the Somerset House Laboratory—
THE CHEMISTRY OF FOODS. With Microscopic
Illustrations.
PART I. TEA, COFFEE, COCOA, SUGAR, ETC. Large crown 8vo, 2s. 6d.
PART II. MILK, BUTTER, CHEESE, CEREALS, PREPARED
STARCHES, ETC. Large crown 8vo, 3s.

BENSON (W.)—
UNIVERSAL PHONOGRAPHY. To classify sounds of
Human Speech, and to denote them by one set of Symbols for easy Writing and
Printing. 8vo, sewed, 1s.
MANUAL OF THE SCIENCE OF COLOUR. Coloured
Frontispiece and Illustrations. 12mo, cloth, 2s. 6d.
PRINCIPLES OF THE SCIENCE OF COLOUR. Small
4to, cloth, 15s.

GHAM (CAPT. THE HON. D.)—
A SELECTION FROM THE LETTERS AND
DESPATCHES OF THE FIRST NAPOLEON. With Explanatory Notes.
3 vols. Demy 8vo, £2 2s.
THE BASTILLE. With Illustrations. 2 vols. Demy 8vo,
32s.
THE MARRIAGES OF THE BOURBONS. 2 vols.
Demy 8vo.   [In the Press.

BIRDWOOD (SIR GEORGE C. M.), C.S.I.—
THE INDUSTRIAL ARTS OF INDIA. With Map and
174 Illustrations. New Edition. Demy 8vo, 14s.

BLACKIE (JOHN STUART), F.R.S.E.—
THE SCOTTISH HIGHLANDERS AND THE LAND
LAWS. Demy 8vo, 9s.
ALTAVONA: FACT AND FICTION FROM MY LIFE
IN THE HIGHLANDS. Third Edition. Crown 8vo, 6s.

BLATHERWICK (CHARLES)—
PERSONAL RECOLLECTIONS OF PETER STONNOR,
Esq. With Illustrations by James Guthrie and A. S. Boyd. Large crown 8vo, 6s.

BLOOMFIELD'S (BENJAMIN LORD), MEMOIR OF—
MISSION TO THE COURT OF BERNADOTTE. Edited by GEORGIANA,
BARONESS BLOOMFIELD, Author of "Reminiscences of Court and Diplomatic Life."
With Portraits. 2 vols. Demy 8vo, 28s.

BROWN (J. MORAY).—
POWDER, SPEAR, AND SPUR: A Sporting Medley.
With Illustrations by G. D. Giles and Edgar Giberne from Sketches by the
Author. Crown 8vo, 10s. 6d.

BURCHETT (R.).—
DEFINITIONS OF GEOMETRY. New Edition. 24mo,
cloth, 5d.

LINEAR PERSPECTIVE, for the Use of Schools of Art.
New Edition. With Illustrations. Post 8vo, cloth, 7s.

PRACTICAL GEOMETRY: The Course of Construction
of Plane Geometrical Figures. With 137 Diagrams. Eighteenth Edition. Post
8vo, cloth, 5s.

BURGESS (EDWARD).—
ENGLISH AND AMERICAN YACHTS. Illustrating
and Describing the most famous Yachts now sailing in English and American
Waters. With a treatise upon Yachts and Yachting. Illustrated with 50 Beautiful
Photogravure Engravings. Oblong folio, £2 2s.

BUTLER (A. J.).—
COURT LIFE IN EGYPT. Second Edition. Illustrated.
Large crown 8vo, 12s.

CARLYLE (THOMAS), WORKS BY.—See pages 29 and 30.
THE CARLYLE BIRTHDAY BOOK. Compiled, with
the permission of Mr. Thomas Carlyle, by C. N. Williamson. Second Edition.
Small fcap. 8vo, 3s.

CHALDÆAN AND ASSYRIAN ART.—
A HISTORY OF ART IN CHALDÆA AND ASSYRIA.
By Georges Perrot and Charles Chipiez. Translated by Walter Armstrong,
B.A. Oxon. With 452 Illustrations. 2 vols. Imperial 8vo, 42s.

CHARNAY (DÉSIRÉ).—
THE ANCIENT CITIES OF THE NEW WORLD.
Being Travels and Explorations in Mexico and Central America, 1857–1882.
Translated from the French by J. Gonino and Helen S. Conant. With upwards of
200 Illustrations. Super Royal 8vo, 31s. 6d.

CHURCH (PROFESSOR A. H.), M.A. Oxon.—
FOOD GRAINS OF INDIA. With numerous Woodcuts.
Small 4to, 6s.

ENGLISH PORCELAIN. A Handbook to the China
made in England during the Eighteenth Century, as Illustrated by Specimens
chiefly in the National Collection. With numerous Woodcuts. Large crown
8vo, 3s.

ENGLISH EARTHENWARE. A Handbook to the
Wares made in England during the 17th and 18th Centuries, as Illustrated by
Specimens in the National Collections. With numerous Woodcuts. Large crown
8vo, 3s.

PLAIN WORDS ABOUT WATER. Illustrated. Crown
8vo, sewed, 6d.

CRAWFURD (OSWALD)—
BEYOND THE SEAS; being the surprising Adventures and ingenious Opinions of Ralph, Lord St. Keyne, told by his kinsman, Humphrey St. Keyne. Second Edition. Crown 8vo, 3s. 6d.

CRIPPS (WILFRED JOSEPH), M.A., F.S.A.—
COLLEGE AND CORPORATION PLATE. A Handbook for the Reproduction of Silver Plate. [*In the South Kensington Museum, from celebrated English collections.*] With numerous Illustrations. Large crown 8vo, cloth, 2s. 6d.

DAIRY FARMING—
DAIRY FARMING. To which is added a Description of the Chief Continental Systems. With numerous Illustrations. By JAMES LONG. Crown 8vo, 9s.

DAIRY FARMING, MANAGEMENT OF COWS, &c. By ARTHUR ROLAND. Edited by WILLIAM ABLETT. Crown 8vo, 5s.

DALY (J. B.), LL.D.—
IRELAND IN THE DAYS OF DEAN SWIFT. Crown 8vo, 5s.

DAUBOURG (E.)—
INTERIOR ARCHITECTURE. Doors, Vestibules, Staircases, Anterooms, Drawing, Dining, and Bed Rooms, Libraries, Bank and Newspaper Offices, Shop Fronts and Interiors. Half-imperial, cloth, £2 12s. 6d.

DAVIDSON (ELLIS A.)—
PRETTY ARTS FOR THE EMPLOYMENT OF LEISURE HOURS. A Book for Ladies. With Illustrations. Demy 8vo, 6s.

DAVITT (MICHAEL)—
LEAVES FROM A PRISON DIARY; or, Lectures to a Solitary Audience. Crown 8vo, 6s.
Cheap Edition. Ninth Thousand. **Crown 8vo, sewed, 1s. 6d.**

DAY (WILLIAM)—
THE RACEHORSE IN TRAINING, with Hints on Racing and Racing Reform, to which is added a Chapter on Shoeing. Sixth Edition. Demy 8vo, 9s.

DAS (DEVENDRA N.)—
SKETCHES OF HINDOO LIFE. Crown 8vo, 5s.

DE AINSLIE (GENERAL)—
A HISTORY OF THE ROYAL REGIMENT OF DRAGOONS. From its Formation in 1661 to the Present Day. With Illustrations. Demy 8vo, 21s.

DE CHAMPEAUX (ALFRED)—
TAPESTRY. With numerous Woodcuts. Cloth, 2s. 6d.

DE FALLOUX (THE COUNT)—
MEMOIRS OF A ROYALIST. Edited by C. B. PITMAN. 2 vols. With Portraits. Demy 8vo, 32s.

D'HAUSSONVILLE (VICOMTE)—
SALON OF MADAME NECKER. Translated by H. M. TROLLOPE. 2 vols. Crown 8vo, 18s.

DREAMS BY A FRENCH FIRESIDE. Translated from the
German by Mary O'Callaghan. Illustrated by Fred Roe. Crown 8vo, 7s. 6d.

DUCOUDRAY (GUSTAVE)—
THE HISTORY OF ANCIENT CIVILISATION. A
Handbook based upon M. Gustave Ducoudray's "Histoire Sommaire de la
Civilisation." Edited by Rev. J. Verschoyle, M.A. With Illustrations. Large
crown 8vo, 6s.

DUFFY (SIR CHARLES GAVAN), K.C.M.G.—
THE LEAGUE OF NORTH AND SOUTH. An Episode
in Irish History, 1850–1854. Crown 8vo, 6s.

DYCE (WILLIAM), R.A.—
DRAWING-BOOK OF THE GOVERNMENT SCHOOL
OF DESIGN ; OR, ELEMENTARY OUTLINES OF ORNAMENT. Fifty
coloured Plates. Folio, sewed, 5s. ; mounted, 18s.
ELEMENTARY OUTLINES OF ORNAMENT. Plates I.
to XXII., containing 97 Examples, adapted for Practice of Standards I. to IV.
Small folio, sewed, 2s. 6d.
SELECTION FROM DYCE'S DRAWING BOOK.
13 Plates, sewed, 1s. 6d. ; mounted on cardboard, 6s. 6d.
TEXT TO ABOVE. Crown 8vo, sewed, 6d.

EDWARDS (H. SUTHERLAND)—
FAMOUS FIRST REPRESENTATIONS. Crown 8vo, 6s.

EGYPTIAN ART—
A HISTORY OF ART IN ANCIENT EGYPT. By
G. Perrot and C. Chipiez. Translated by Walter Armstrong. With over
600 Illustrations. 2 vols. Imperial 8vo, £2 2s.

ELLIS (A. B., Major 1st West India Regiment)—
WEST AFRICAN STORIES. Crown 8vo.
THE TSHI-SPEAKING PEOPLES OF THE GOLD
COAST OF WEST AFRICA: their Religion, Manners, Customs, Laws,
Language, &c. With Map. Demy 8vo, 10s. 6d.
SOUTH AFRICAN SKETCHES. Crown 8vo, 6s.
WEST AFRICAN ISLANDS. Demy 8vo, 14s.
THE HISTORY OF THE WEST INDIA REGI-
MENT. With Maps and Coloured Frontispiece and Title-page. Demy 8vo, 18s.
THE LAND OF FETISH. Demy 8vo, 12s.

ENGEL (CARL)—
MUSICAL INSTRUMENTS. With numerous Woodcuts.
Large crown 8vo, cloth, 2s. 6d.

ESCOTT (T. H. S.)—
POLITICS AND LETTERS. Demy 8vo, 9s.
ENGLAND. ITS PEOPLE, POLITY, AND PURSUITS.
New and Revised Edition. Sixth Thousand. 8vo, 8s.
EUROPEAN POLITICS, THE PRESENT POSITION OF.
By the Author of "Greater Britain." Demy 8vo, 10s.

FANE (VIOLET)—
QUEEN OF THE FAIRIES (A Village Story), and other
Poems. Crown 8vo, 6s.
ANTHONY BABINGTON : a Drama. Crown 8vo, 6s.

FORTNUM (C. D. E.), F.S.A.—
  MAIOLICA. With numerous Woodcuts. Large crown
  8vo, cloth, 2s. 6d.
  BRONZES. With numerous Woodcuts. Large crown
  8vo, cloth, 2s. 6d.
FOUQUÉ (DE LA MOTTE)—
  UNDINE : a Romance translated from the German. With
  an Introduction by JULIA CARTWRIGHT. Illustrated by HEYWOOD SUMNER.
  Crown 4to. 3s.
FRANCATELLI (C. E.)—
  THE ROYAL CONFECTIONER : English and Foreign.
  A Practical Treatise. With Illustrations. Fifth Edition. Crown 8vo, 5s.
FRANCIS (FRANCIS, JUNR.
  SADDLE AND MOCASSIN. 8vo, 12s.
FRANKS (A. W.)—
  JAPANESE POTTERY. Being a Native Report, with an
  Introduction and Catalogue. With numerous Illustrations and Marks. Large
  crown 8vo, cloth, 2s. 6d.
  FROBEL, FRIEDRICH ; a Short Sketch of his Life, including
  Froebel's Letters from Dresden and Leipzig to his Wife, now first Translated into
  English. By EMILY SHIRREFF. Crown 8vo, 2s.
  GALILEO AND HIS JUDGES. By F. R. WEGG-PROSSER.
  Demy 8vo, 7s.
GALLENGA (ANTONIO)—
  ITALY: PRESENT AND FUTURE. 2 vols. Dmy. 8vo, 21s.
  EPISODES OF MY SECOND LIFE. 2 vols. Dmy. 8vo, 28s.
  IBERIAN REMINISCENCES. Fifteen Years' Travelling
  Impressions of Spain and Portugal. With a Map. 2 vols. Demy 8vo, 32s.
GASNAULT (PAUL) and GARNIER (ED.)—
  FRENCH POTTERY. With Illustrations and Marks.
  Large crown 8vo, 3s.
GILLMORE (PARKER)—
  THE HUNTER'S ARCADIA. With numerous Illustra-
  tions. Demy 8vo, 10s. 6d.
  GIRL'S LIFE EIGHTY YEARS AGO (A). Selections from
  the Letters of Eliza Southgate Bowne, with an Introduction by Clarence Cook.
  Illustrated with Portraits and Views. Crown 4to, 12s.
GLEICHEN (COUNT), Grenadier Guards—
  WITH THE CAMEL CORPS UP THE NILE. With
  numerous Sketches by the Author. Third Edition. Large crown 8vo, 9s.
GORDON (GENERAL)—
  LETTERS FROM THE CRIMEA, THE DANUBE,
  AND ARMENIA. Edited by DEMETRIUS C. BOULGER. Second Edition.
  Crown 8vo, 5s.
GORST (SIR J. E.), Q.C., M.P.—
  An ELECTION MANUAL. Containing the Parliamentary
  Elections (Corrupt and Illegal Practices) Act, 1883, with Notes. Third Edition.
  Crown 8vo, 1s. 6d.
GOWER (A. R.), Royal School of Mines—
  PRACTICAL METALLURGY. With Illustrations. Crown
  8vo, 3s.
GRAHAM (SIR GERALD), V.C., K.C.B.—
  LAST WORDS WITH GORDON. Crown 8vo, cloth, 1s.

HOPE (ANDRÉE)—
CHRONICLES OF AN OLD INN; or, a Few Words about Gray's Inn. Crown 8vo, 3s.

HOVELACQUE (ABEL)—
THE SCIENCE OF LANGUAGE: LINGUISTICS, PHILOLOGY, AND ETYMOLOGY. With Maps. Large crown 8vo, cloth, 5s.

HOZIER (H. M.)—
TURENNE. With Portrait and Two Maps. Large crown 8vo, 4s.

HUEFFER (F.)—
HALF A CENTURY OF MUSIC IN ENGLAND. 1837—1887. Demy 8vo.

NUMPHRIS (H. D.)—
PRINCIPLES OF PERSPECTIVE. Illustrated in a Series of Examples. Oblong folio, half-bound, and Text 8vo, cloth, £1 1s.

HUNTLY (MARQUIS OF)—
TRAVELS, SPORTS, AND POLITICS IN THE EAST OF EUROPE. With Illustrations by the Marchioness of Huntly. Large Crown 8vo, 12s.

INDUSTRIAL ARTS: Historical Sketches. With numerous Illustrations. Large crown 8vo, 3s.

INTERNATIONAL POLICY: Essay on the Foreign Relations of England. By Frederic Harrison, Prof. Beesley, Richard Congreve, and others. New Edition. Crown 8vo, 2s. 6d.

IRELAND IN THE DAYS OF DEAN SWIFT. By J. B. Daly, LL.D. Crown 8vo, 5s.

IRISH ART OF LACEMAKING, A RENASCENCE OF THE. Illustrated by Photographic Reproductions of Irish Laces, made from new and specially designed Patterns. Introductory Notes and Descriptions. By A. S. C. Demy 8vo, 2s. 6d.

IRON (RALPH), (OLIVE SCHREINER)—
THE STORY OF AN AFRICAN FARM. New Edition. Crown 8vo, 2s.; in cloth, 2s.

JACKSON (FRANK G.), Master in the Birmingham Municipal School of Art—
DECORATIVE DESIGN. An Elementary Text Book of Principles and Practice. With numerous Illustrations. Crown 8vo, 7s. 6d.

JAMES (HENRY A.)—
HANDBOOK TO PERSPECTIVE. Crown 8vo, 2s. 6d.

JARRY (GENERAL)—
OUTPOST DUTY. Translated, with TREATISES ON MILITARY RECONNAISANCE AND ON ROAD-MAKING. By Major-Gen. W. C. E. Napier. Third Edition. Crown 8vo, 5s.

JEANS (W. T.)—
CREATORS OF THE AGE OF STEEL. Memoirs of Sir W. Siemens, Sir H. Bessemer, Sir J. Whitworth, Sir J. Brown, and other Inventors. Second Edition. Crown 8vo, 7s. 6d.

JOHNSON (DR. SAMUEL)—
LIFE AND CONVERSATIONS OF DR. SAMUEL JOHNSON. By A. Main. Crown 8vo, 10s. 6d.

LEFÈVRE (ANDRÉ)—
  PHILOSOPHY, Historical and Critical. Translated, with
    an Introduction, by A. W. Keane, B.A. Large crown 8vo, 7s. 6d.
LESLIE (R. C.)—
  LIFE ABOARD A BRITISH PRIVATEER IN THE
    TIME OF QUEEN ANNE. Being the Journals of Captain Woodes Rogers,
    Master Mariner. With Notes and Illustrations by Robert C. Leslie. Large
    crown 8vo, 3s.
  A SEA PAINTER'S LOG. With 12 Full-page Illustrations
    by the Author. Large crown 8vo, 12s.
LETOURNEAU (DR. CHARLES)—
  SOCIOLOGY. Based upon Ethnology. Large crown
    8vo, 10s.
  BIOLOGY. Translated by William MacCall. With Illus-
    trations. Large crown 8vo, 6s.
LILLY (W. S.)—
  CHAPTERS ON EUROPEAN HISTORY. With an
    Introductory Dialogue on the Philosophy of History. 2 vols. Demy 8vo, 21s.
  ANCIENT RELIGION AND MODERN THOUGHT.
    Third Edition, revised, with additions. Demy 8vo, 12s.
LITTLE (THE REV. CANON KNOX)—
  THE CHILD OF STAFFERTON: A Chapter from a
    Family Chronicle. Tenth Thousand. Crown 8vo, 2s. 6d.
  THE BROKEN VOW. A Story of Here and Hereafter.
    Tenth Thousand. Crown 8vo, 2s. 6d.
*LLOYD (COLONEL E.M.), R.E., late Professor of Fortification at the Royal
  Military Academy, Woolwich—*
  VAUBAN, MONTALEMBERT, CARNOT: ENGINEER
    STUDIES. With Portraits. Crown 8vo, 5s
LONG (JAMES)—
  DAIRY FARMING. To which is added a Description of
    the Chief Continental Systems. With numerous Illustrations. Crown 8vo, 9s.
LOW (C. R.)—
  SOLDIERS OF THE VICTORIAN AGE. 2 vols. Demy
    8vo, £1 10s.
LOW (WILLIAM)—
  TABLE DECORATION. With 19 Full Illustrations.
    Demy 8vo, 6s.
LYTTON (ROBERT, EARL)—
  POETICAL WORKS—
    FABLES IN SONG. 2 vols. Fcap. 8vo, 12s.
    THE WANDERER. Fcap. 8vo, 6s.
    POEMS, HISTORICAL AND CHARACTERISTIC. Fcap. 6s.

MERIVALE (HERMAN CHARLES)—
 BINKO'S BLUES. A Tale for Children of all Growths.
 Illustrated by EDGAR GIBERNE. Small crown 8vo, 3s.

 THE WHITE PILGRIM, and other Poems. Crown 8vo, 9s.

MOLESWORTH (W. NASSAU)—
 HISTORY OF ENGLAND FROM THE YEAR 1830
 TO THE RESIGNATION OF THE GLADSTONE MINISTRY, 1874.
 Twelfth Thousand. 3 vols. Crown 8vo, 18s.
 ABRIDGED EDITION. Large crown, 7s. 6d.

MOLTKE (FIELD-MARSHAL COUNT VON)—
 POLAND : AN HISTORICAL SKETCH. An Authorised
 Translation, with Biographical Notice by E. S. BUCKHEIM. Crown 8vo, 4s. 6d.

MORLEY (THE RIGHT HON. JOHN), M.P.—
 RICHARD COBDEN'S LIFE AND CORRESPON-
 DENCE. Crown 8vo, with Portrait, 7s. 6d.
 Popular Edition. With Portrait. 4to, sewed, 1s. Cloth, 2s.

MUNTZ (EUGENE)—
 RAPHAEL : his Life, Works, and Times. Illustrated with
 about 200 Engravings. A new Edition, revised from the Second French Edition
 by W. ARMSTRONG, B.A. Oxon. Imperial 8vo, 25s.

MURRAY (ANDREW), F.L.S.—
 ECONOMIC ENTOMOLOGY. APTERA. With numerous Illustrations. Large crown 8vo, 7s. 6d.

NAPIER (MAJ.-GEN. W. C. E.)—
 TRANSLATION OF GEN. JARRY'S OUTPOST DUTY.
 With TREATISES ON MILITARY RECONNAISSANCE AND ON
 ROAD-MAKING. Third Edition. Crown 8vo, 5s.

 NAPOLEON. A Selection from the Letters and Despatches of
 the First Napoleon. With Explanatory Notes by Captain the Hon. D. BINGHAM.
 3 vols. Demy 8vo, £2 2s.

NECKER (MADAME)—
 THE SALON OF MADAME NECKER. By VICOMTE
 D'HAUSSONVILLE. 2 vols. Crown 8vo, 18s.

NESBITT (ALEXANDER)—
 GLASS. With numerous Woodcuts. Large crown 8vo,
 cloth, 2s. 6d.

NEVINSON (HENRY)—
 A SKETCH OF HERDER AND HIS TIMES. With
 a Portrait. Demy 8vo, 14s.

PETERBOROUGH (THE EARL OF)—
THE EARL OF PETERBOROUGH AND MON-
MOUTH (Charles Mordaunt): A Memoir. By Colonel Frank Russell, Royal
Dragoons. With Illustrations. 2 vols. demy 8vo. 30s.

PHŒNICIAN ART—
A HISTORY OF ANCIENT ART IN PHŒNICIA
AND ITS DEPENDENCIES. By George Perrot and Charles Chipiez.
Translated from the French by Walter Armstrong, B.A. Oxon. Containing
644 Illustrations in the text, and 10 Steel and Coloured Plates. 2 vols. Imperial
8vo, 42s.

PITT TAYLOR (FRANK)—
THE CANTERBURY TALES. Selections from the Tales
of Geoffrey Chaucer rendered into Modern English, with close adherence
to the language of the Poet. With Frontispiece. Crown 8vo, 6s.

POLLEN (J. H.)—
GOLD AND SILVER SMITH'S WORK. With numerous Woodcuts. Large crown 8vo, cloth, 2s. 6d.

ANCIENT AND MODERN FURNITURE AND
WOODWORK. With numerous Woodcuts. Large crown 8vo, cloth, 2s. 6d.

POOLE (STANLEY LANE), B.A., M.R.A.S.—
THE ART OF THE SARACENS IN EGYPT. Pub-
lished for the Committee of Council on Education. With 108 Woodcuts. Large
crown 8vo, 4s.

POYNTER (E. J.), R.A.—
TEN LECTURES ON ART. Third Edition. Large
crown 8vo, 9s.

PRINSEP (VAL), A.R.A.—
IMPERIAL INDIA. Containing numerous Illustrations
and Maps. Second Edition. Demy 8vo, £1 1s.

RADICAL PROGRAMME, THE. From the *Fortnightly
Review*, with additions. With a Preface by the Right Hon. J. Chamberlain,
M.P. Thirteenth Thousand. Crown 8vo, 2s. 6d.

RAE (W. FRASER)—
AUSTRIAN HEALTH RESORTS : and the Bitter Waters
of Hungary. Crown 8vo, 9s.

RAMSDEN (LADY GWENDOLEN)—
A BIRTHDAY BOOK. Illustrated. Containing 46 Illustra-
tions from Original Drawings, and numerous other Illustrations. Royal 8vo, 21s.

RAPHAEL : his Life, Works, and Times. By Eugène Müntz.
Illustrated with about 200 Engravings. A New Edition, revised from the Second
French Edition. By W. Armstrong, B.A. Imperial 8vo, 25s.

REDGRAVE (GILBERT)—
OUTLINES OF HISTORIC ORNAMENT. Translated
from the German. Edited by Gilbert Redgrave. With numerous Illustrations.
Crown 8vo, 4s.

REDGRAVE (GILBERT R.)—
MANUAL OF DESIGN, compiled from the Writings and
Addresses of Richard Redgrave, R.A. With Woodcuts. Large crown 8vo, cloth,
2s. 6d.

REDGRAVE (RICHARD)—
ELEMENTARY MANUAL OF COLOUR, with a
Catechism on Colour. 24mo, cloth, 9d.

REDGRAVE (SAMUEL)—
A DESCRIPTIVE CATALOGUE OF THE HIS-
TORICAL COLLECTION OF WATER-COLOUR PAINTINGS IN THE
SOUTH KENSINGTON MUSEUM. With numerous Chromo-lithographs and
other Illustrations. Royal 8vo, £1 1s.

REID (T. WEMYSS)—
THE LIFE OF THE RIGHT HON. W. E. FORSTER.
With Portraits. Fourth Edition. 2 vols. Demy 8vo, 32s.
FIFTH EDITION, in one volume, with new Portrait. Demy 8vo, 10s. 6d.

RENAN (ERNEST)—
HISTORY OF THE PEOPLE OF ISRAEL TILL THE
TIME OF KING DAVID. Demy 8vo, 14s.

HISTORY OF THE PEOPLE OF ISRAEL. From the
Reign of David up to the Capture of Samaria. Second Division. Demy 8vo, 14s.

RECOLLECTIONS OF MY YOUTH. Translated from
the original French, and revised by Madame Renan. Crown 8vo, 8s.

REYNARDSON (C. T. S. BIRCH)—
SPORTS AND ANECDOTES OF BYGONE DAYS
in England, Scotland, Ireland, Italy, and the Sunny South. With numerous
Illustrations in Colour. Large crown 8vo, 21s.

DOWN THE ROAD : Reminiscences of a Gentleman
Coachman. With Coloured Illustrations. Large crown 8vo, 21s.

RIANO (JUAN F.)—
THE INDUSTRIAL ARTS IN SPAIN. With numerous
Woodcuts. Large crown 8vo, cloth, 4s.

RIBTON-TURNER (C. J.)—
A HISTORY OF VAGRANTS AND VAGRANCY AND BEGGARS AND BEGGING. With Illustrations. Demy 8vo, 21s.

ROBINSON (JAMES F.)—
BRITISH BEE FARMING. Its Profits and Pleasures. Large crown 8vo, 5s.

ROBINSON (J. C.)—
ITALIAN SCULPTURE OF THE MIDDLE AGES AND PERIOD OF THE REVIVAL OF ART. With 20 Engravings. Royal 8vo, cloth, 7s. 6d.

ROBSON (GEORGE)—
ELEMENTARY BUILDING CONSTRUCTION. Illustrated by a Design for an Entrance Lodge and Gate. 15 Plates. Oblong folio, sewed, 8s.

ROBSON (REV. J. H.), M.A., LL.M.—
AN ELEMENTARY TREATISE ON ALGEBRA. Post 8vo, 6s.

ROCK (THE VERY REV. CANON), D.D.—
TEXTILE FABRICS. With numerous Woodcuts. Large crown 8vo, cloth, 2s. 6d.

ROGERS (CAPTAIN WOODES), Master Mariner—
LIFE ABOARD A BRITISH PRIVATEER IN THE TIME OF QUEEN ANNE. Being the Journals of Captain Woodes Rogers, Master Mariner. With Notes and Illustrations by ROBERT C. LESLIE, Author of "A Sea Painter's Log." Large crown 8vo, 5s.

ROOSE (ROBSON), M.D., F.C.S.—
THE WEAR AND TEAR OF LONDON LIFE. Second Edition. Crown 8vo, sewed, 1s.
INFECTION AND DISINFECTION. Crown 8vo, sewed, 6d.

ROLAND (ARTHUR)—
FARMING FOR PLEASURE AND PROFIT. Edited by WILLIAM ABLETT. 8 vols. Crown 8vo, 5s. each.
DAIRY-FARMING, MANAGEMENT OF COWS, &c.
POULTRY-KEEPING.
TREE-PLANTING, FOR ORNAMENTATION OR PROFIT.
STOCK-KEEPING AND CATTLE-REARING.
DRAINAGE OF LAND, IRRIGATION, MANURES, &c.
ROOT-GROWING, HOPS, &c.
MANAGEMENT OF GRASS LANDS, LAYING DOWN GRASS, ARTIFICIAL GRASSES, &c.
MARKET GARDENING, HUSBANDRY FOR FARMERS AND GENERAL CULTIVATORS.

SIMMONDS (T. L.)—
ANIMAL PRODUCTS: their Preparation, Commercial Uses, and Value. With numerous Illustrations. Large crown 8vo, 7s. 6d.

SINGER'S STORY, A. Related by the Author of "Flitters, Tatters, and the Counsellor." Crown 8vo, sewed, 1s.

SINNETT (A. P.)—
ESOTERIC BUDDHISM. Annotated and enlarged by the Author. Sixth and cheaper Edition. Crown 8vo, 4s.

KARMA. A Novel. New Edition. Crown 8vo, 3s. 6d.

SINNETT (MRS.)—
THE PURPOSE OF THEOSOPHY. Crown 8vo, 3s.

SMITH (ALEXANDER SKENE)—
HOLIDAY RECREATIONS, AND OTHER POEMS. With a Preface by Rev. Principal Cairns, D.D. Crown 8vo, 3s.

SMITH (MAJOR R. MURDOCK), R.E.—
PERSIAN ART. With Map and Woodcuts. Second Edition. Large crown 8vo, 2s.

STOKES (MARGARET)—
EARLY CHRISTIAN ART IN IRELAND. With 106 Woodcuts. Demy 8vo, 7s. 6d.

STORY (W. W.)—
ROBA DI ROMA. Seventh Edition, with Additions and Portraits. Crown 8vo, cloth, 10s. 6d.

CASTLE ST. ANGELO. With Illustrations. Crown 8vo, 10s. 6d.

A SUBURB OF YEDO. By T. A. P. With Illustrations. Crown 8vo.

SUTCLIFFE (JOHN)—
THE SCULPTOR AND ART STUDENT'S GUIDE to the Proportions of the Human Form, with Measurements in feet and inches of Full-Grown Figures of Both Sexes and of Various Ages. By Dr. G. Schadow, Member of the Academies, Stockholm, Dresden, Rome, &c. &c. Translated by J. J. Wright. Plates reproduced by J. Sutcliffe. Oblong folio, 31s. 6d.

TAINE (H. A.)—
NOTES ON ENGLAND. Translated, with Introduction, by W. Fraser Rae. Eighth Edition. With Portrait. Crown 8vo, 5s.

TANNER (PROFESSOR), F.C.S.—
HOLT CASTLE; or, Threefold Interest in Land. Crown 8vo, 4s. 6d.

JACK'S EDUCATION; OR, HOW HE LEARNT FARMING. Second Edition. Crown 8vo, 3s. 6d.

WARING (CHARLES)—
STATE PURCHASE OF RAILWAYS. Demy 8vo, 5s.

WATSON (WILLIAM)—
LIFE IN THE CONFEDERATE ARMY; being the
Observations and Experiences of an Alien in the South during the American Civil
War. Crown 8vo, 8s.

WEGG-PROSSER (F. R.)—
GALILEO AND HIS JUDGES. Demy 8vo, 5s.

WHITE (WALTER)—
A MONTH IN YORKSHIRE. With a Map. Fifth
Edition. Post 8vo, 4s.

A LONDONER'S WALK TO THE LAND'S END, AND
A TRIP TO THE SCILLY ISLES. With 4 Maps. Third Edition. Post
8vo, 4s.

WILL-O'-THE-WISPS, THE. Translated from the German
of Marie Petersen by CHARLOTTE J. HART. With Illustrations. Crown 8vo,
7s. 6d.

WORKING MAN'S PHILOSOPHY, A. By "ONE OF THE
CROWD." Crown 8vo, 3s.

WORNUM (R. N.)—
ANALYSIS OF ORNAMENT: THE CHARACTER-
ISTICS OF STYLES. An Introduction to the History of Ornamental Art.
With many Illustrations. Ninth Edition. Royal 8vo, cloth, 8s.

WRIGHTSON (PROF. JOHN), M.R.A.C., F.C.S., &c.; Examiner in
Agriculture to the Science and Art Department; Professor of Agriculture in
the Normal School of Science and Royal School of Mines; President of the
College of Agriculture, Downton, near Salisbury; late Commissioner for the
Royal Agricultural Society of England, &c., &c.

PRINCIPLES OF AGRICULTURAL PRACTICE AS
AN INSTRUCTIONAL SUBJECT. With Geological Map. Crown 8vo, 5s.

FALLOW AND FODDER CROPS. [*In the Press.*

WORSAAE (J. J. A.)—
INDUSTRIAL ARTS OF DENMARK, FROM THE
EARLIEST TIMES TO THE DANISH CONQUEST OF ENGLAND.
With Maps and Woodcuts. Large crown 8vo, 3s. 6d.

YEO (DR. J. BURNEY)—
CLIMATE AND HEALTH RESORTS. New Edition.
Crown 8vo, 10s. 6d.

YOUNGE (C. D.)—
PARALLEL LIVES OF ANCIENT AND MODERN
HEROES. New Edition. 12mo, cloth, 4s. 6d.

WINDT (H. DE)—
FROM CALAIS TO PEKIN BY LAND. With
Numerous Illustrations by the Author. Demy 8vo.

YOUNG OFFICER'S "DON'T"; or, Hints to Youngsters
on Joining. 32mo. 1s.

28 BOOKS PUBLISHED BY

SOUTH KENSINGTON MUSEUM SCIENCE & ART HANDBOOKS—*Continued.*

PLAIN WORDS ABOUT WATER. By A. H. CHURCH, M.A. Oxon. With Illustrations. Sewed, 6d.

ANIMAL PRODUCTS: their Preparation, Commercial Uses, and Value. By T. L. SIMMONDS. With Illustrations. 7s. 6d.

FOOD: Some Account of its Sources, Constituents, and Uses. By PROFESSOR A. H. CHURCH, M.A. Oxon. Sixth Thousand. 3s.

ECONOMIC ENTOMOLOGY. By ANDREW MURRAY, F.L.S. APTERA. With Illustrations. 7s. 6d.

JAPANESE POTTERY. Being a Native Report. With an Introduction and Catalogue by A. W. FRANKS, M.A., F.R.S., F.S.A. With Illustrations and Marks. 2s. 6d.

HANDBOOK TO THE SPECIAL LOAN COLLECTION of Scientific Apparatus. 3s.

INDUSTRIAL ARTS: Historical Sketches. With Numerous Illustrations. 3s.

TEXTILE FABRICS. By the Very Rev. DANIEL ROCK, D.D. With numerous Woodcuts. 2s. 6d.

JONES COLLECTION IN THE SOUTH KENSINGTON MUSEUM. With Portrait and Woodcuts. 2s. 6d.

COLLEGE AND CORPORATION PLATE. A Handbook to the Reproductions of Silver Plate in the South Kensington Museum from Celebrated English Collections. By WILFRED JOSEPH CRIPPS, M.A., F.S.A. With Illustrations. 2s. 6d.

IVORIES: ANCIENT AND MEDIÆVAL. By WILLIAM MASKELL. With numerous Woodcuts. 2s. 6d.

ANCIENT AND MODERN FURNITURE AND WOOD-WORK. By JOHN HUNGERFORD POLLEN, M.A. With numerous Woodcuts. 2s. 6d.

MAIOLICA. By C. DRURY E. FORTNUM, F.S.A. With numerous Woodcuts. 2s. 6d.

THE CHEMISTRY OF FOODS. With Microscopic Illustrations. By JAMES BELL, Ph.D., &c., Principal of the Somerset House Laboratory. Part I.—Tea, Coffee, Cocoa, Sugar, &c. 2s. 6d. Part II.—Milk, Butter, Cheese, Cereals, Prepared Starches, &c. 3s.

MUSICAL INSTRUMENTS. By CARL ENGEL. With numerous Woodcuts. 2s. 6d.

MANUAL OF DESIGN, compiled from the Writings and Addresses of RICHARD REDGRAVE, R.A. By GILBERT R. REDGRAVE. With Woodcuts. 2s. 6d.

PERSIAN ART. By MAJOR R. MURDOCK SMITH, R.E. With Map and Woodcuts. Second Edition, enlarged. 2s.

CHEAP AND UNIFORM EDITION.

23 vols., Crown 8vo, cloth, £7 5s.

THE FRENCH REVOLUTION:
A History. 2 vols., 12s.

OLIVER CROMWELL'S LET-
TERS AND SPEECHES, with Eluci-
dations, &c. 3 vols., 18s.

LIVES OF SCHILLER AND
JOHN STERLING. 1 vol., 6s.

CRITICAL AND MISCELLA-
NEOUS ESSAYS. 4 vols., £1 4s.

SARTOR RESARTUS AND
LECTURES ON HEROES. 1 vol., 6s.

LATTER-DAY PAMPHLETS.
1 vol., 6s.

CHARTISM AND PAST AND
PRESENT. 1 vol., 6s.

TRANSLATIONS FROM THE
GERMAN OF MUSÆUS, TIECK,
AND RICHTER. 2 vols., 6s.

WILHELM MEISTER, by Göethe.
A Translation. 2 vols., 12s.

HISTORY OF FRIEDRICH THE
SECOND, called Frederick the Great.
7 vols., £3 9s.

PEOPLE'S EDITION.

37 vols., small crown 8vo, 37s.; separate vols., 1s. each.

SARTOR RESARTUS. With Portrait of Thomas Carlyle.

FRENCH REVOLUTION. A
History. 3 vols.

OLIVER CROMWELL'S LET-
TERS AND SPEECHES. 5 vols.
With Portrait of Oliver Cromwell.

ON HEROES AND HERO
WORSHIP, AND THE HEROIC
IN HISTORY.

PAST AND PRESENT.

CRITICAL AND MISCELLA-
NEOUS ESSAYS. 7 vols.

THE LIFE OF SCHILLER,
AND EXAMINATION OF HIS
WORKS. With Portrait.

LATTER-DAY PAMPHLETS.

WILHELM MEISTER. 3 vols.

LIFE OF JOHN STERLING.
With Portrait.

HISTORY OF FREDERICK
THE GREAT. 10 vols.

TRANSLATIONS FROM
MUSÆUS, TIECK, AND RICHTER.
2 vols.

THE EARLY KINGS OF NOR-
WAY; Essay on the Portraits of Knox.

Sets, 37 vols. in 18, 37s.

CHEAP ISSUE.

THE FRENCH REVOLUTION. Complete in 1 vol. With Portrait.
Crown 8vo, 2s.

SARTOR RESARTUS, HEROES AND HERO WORSHIP, PAST
AND PRESENT, AND CHARTISM. Complete in 1 vol. Crown 8vo, 2s.

OLIVER CROMWELL'S LETTERS AND SPEECHES. Crown 8vo,
2s. 6d.

CRITICAL AND MISCELLANEOUS ESSAYS. 2 vols. 4s.

SIXPENNY EDITION.

4to, sewed.

SARTOR RESARTUS. Eightieth Thousand.

HEROES AND HERO WORSHIP.

ESSAYS: BURNS, JOHNSON, SCOTT, THE DIAMOND NECKLACE.

The above in 1 vol., cloth, 2s. 6d.

DICKENS'S (CHARLES) WORKS.—*Continued.*

LIBRARY EDITION.

In post 8vo.   With the Original Illustrations, 30 vols., cloth, £12.

		s.	d.
PICKWICK PAPERS	43 Illustrns., 2 vols.	16	0
NICHOLAS NICKLEBY	39 " 2 vols.	16	0
MARTIN CHUZZLEWIT	40 " 2 vols.	16	0
OLD CURIOSITY SHOP & REPRINTED PIECES	36 " 2 vols.	16	0
BARNABY RUDGE and HARD TIMES	36 " 2 vols.	16	0
BLEAK HOUSE	40 " 2 vols.	16	0
LITTLE DORRIT	40 " 2 vols.	16	0
DOMBEY AND SON	38 " 2 vols.	16	0
DAVID COPPERFIELD	38 " 2 vols.	16	0
OUR MUTUAL FRIEND	40 " 2 vols.	16	0
SKETCHES BY "BOZ"	39 " 1 vol.	8	0
OLIVER TWIST	24 " 1 vol.	8	0
CHRISTMAS BOOKS	17 " 1 vol.	8	0
A TALE OF TWO CITIES	16 " 1 vol.	8	0
GREAT EXPECTATIONS	8 " 1 vol.	8	0
PICTURES FROM ITALY & AMERICAN NOTES	8 " 1 vol.	8	0
UNCOMMERCIAL TRAVELLER	8 " 1 vol.	8	0
CHILD'S HISTORY OF ENGLAND	8 " 1 vol.	8	0
EDWIN DROOD and MISCELLANIES	12 " 1 vol.	8	0
CHRISTMAS STORIES from "Household Words," &c.	14 " 1 vol.	8	0

THE LIFE OF CHARLES DICKENS. By JOHN FORSTER. With Illustrations. Uniform with this Edition. 10s. 6d.

A NEW EDITION OF ABOVE, WITH THE ORIGINAL ILLUSTRATIONS, IN LARGE CROWN 8vo, 30 VOLS. IN SETS ONLY.

THE "CHARLES DICKENS" EDITION.

In Crown 8vo.   In 21 vols., cloth, with Illustrations, £3 16s.

		s.	d.
PICKWICK PAPERS	8 Illustrations	4	0
MARTIN CHUZZLEWIT	8 "	4	0
DOMBEY AND SON	8 "	4	0
NICHOLAS NICKLEBY	8 "	4	0
DAVID COPPERFIELD	8 "	4	0
BLEAK HOUSE	8 "	4	0
LITTLE DORRIT	8 "	4	0
OUR MUTUAL FRIEND	8 "	4	0
BARNABY RUDGE	8 "	4	0
OLD CURIOSITY SHOP	8 "	3	6
A CHILD'S HISTORY OF ENGLAND	8 "	3	6
EDWIN DROOD and OTHER STORIES	8 "	3	6
CHRISTMAS STORIES, from "Household Words"	8 "	3	6
SKETCHES BY "BOZ"	8 "	3	6
AMERICAN NOTES and REPRINTED PIECES	8 "	3	6
CHRISTMAS BOOKS	8 "	3	6
OLIVER TWIST	8 "	3	6
GREAT EXPECTATIONS	8 "	3	6
TALE OF TWO CITIES	8 "	3	0
HARD TIMES and PICTURES FROM ITALY	8 "	3	0
UNCOMMERCIAL TRAVELLER	8 "	3	0
THE LIFE OF CHARLES DICKENS. Numerous Illustrations.	2 vols.	7	0
THE LETTERS OF CHARLES DICKENS	2 vols.	7	0

DICKENS'S (CHARLES) WORKS.—*Continued.*

THE POPULAR LIBRARY EDITION
OF THE WORKS OF
CHARLES DICKENS,

In 30 Vols., large crown 8vo, price £6; separate Vols. 4s. each.

An Edition printed on good paper, each volume containing 16 full-page Illustrations, selected from the Household Edition, on Plate Paper.

SKETCHES BY "BOZ."
PICKWICK. 2 vols.
OLIVER TWIST.
NICHOLAS NICKLEBY 2 vols.
MARTIN CHUZZLEWIT. 2 vols.
DOMBEY AND SON. 2 vols.
DAVID COPPERFIELD. 2 vols.
CHRISTMAS BOOKS.
OUR MUTUAL FRIEND. 2 vols.
CHRISTMAS STORIES.
BLEAK HOUSE. 2 vols.
LITTLE DORRIT. 2 vols.
OLD CURIOSITY SHOP AND REPRINTED PIECES. 2 vols
BARNABY RUDGE. 2 vols. .
UNCOMMERCIAL TRAVELLER.
GREAT EXPECTATIONS.
TALE OF TWO CITIES.
CHILD'S HISTORY OF ENGLAND.
EDWIN DROOD AND MISCELLANIES.
PICTURES FROM ITALY AND AMERICAN NOTES,

DICKENS'S (CHARLES) WORKS.—*Continued.*

THE CABINET EDITION.

In 32 vols. small fcap. 8vo, Marble Paper Sides, Cloth Backs, with uncut edges, price Eighteenpence each.

Each Volume contains Eight Illustrations reproduced from the Originals.

CHRISTMAS BOOKS.
MARTIN CHUZZLEWIT, Two Vols.
DAVID COPPERFIELD, Two Vols.
OLIVER TWIST.
GREAT EXPECTATIONS.
NICHOLAS NICKLEBY, Two Vols.
SKETCHES BY "BOZ."
CHRISTMAS STORIES.
THE PICKWICK PAPERS, Two Vols.
BARNABY RUDGE, Two Vols.
BLEAK HOUSE, Two Vols.
AMERICAN NOTES AND PICTURES FROM ITALY.
EDWIN DROOD; AND OTHER STORIES.
THE OLD CURIOSITY SHOP, Two Vols.
A CHILD'S HISTORY OF ENGLAND
DOMBEY AND SON, Two Vols.
A TALE OF TWO CITIES.
LITTLE DORRIT, Two Vols.
MUTUAL FRIEND, Two Vols.
HARD TIMES.
UNCOMMERCIAL TRAVELLER.
REPRINTED PIECES.

NEW & CHEAP ISSUE OF THE WORKS OF CHARLES DICKENS.

In Pocket Volumes.

PICKWICK PAPERS, with 8 Illustrations, cloth, 2s.
NICHOLAS NICKLEBY, with 8 Illustrations, cloth, 2s.
OLIVER TWIST, with 8 Illustrations, cloth, 1s.
SKETCHES BY "BOZ," with 8 Illustrations, cloth, 2s.
OLD CURIOSITY SHOP, with 8 Illustrations, cloth, 2s.
BARNABY RUDGE, with 16 Illustrations, cloth, 2s.
AMERICAN NOTES AND PICTURES FROM ITALY, with
    8 Illustrations, cloth, 1s. 6d.
CHRISTMAS BOOKS, with 8 Illustrations, cloth, 1s. 6d.
MARTIN CHUZZLEWIT, with 8 Illustrations, 2s.

SCIENCE AND ART,

A Journal for Teachers and Students.

ISSUED BY Messrs. CHAPMAN & HALL, Limited,

Agents for the Science and Art Department of the Committee of Council on Education.

MONTHLY, PRICE THREEPENCE.

The Journal contains contributions by distinguished men ; short papers by prominent teachers ; leading articles ; correspondence ; answers to questions set at the May Examinations of the Science and Art Department ; and interesting news in connection with the scientific and artistic world.

PRIZE COMPETITION.

With each Issue of the Journal, papers or drawings are offered for Prize Competition, extending over the range of subjects of the Science and Art Department and City and Guilds of London Institute.

There are thousands of Science and Art Schools and Classes in the United Kingdom, but the teachers connected with these institutions, although engaged in the advancement of identical objects, are seldom known to each other except through personal friendship. One object of the new Journal is to enable those engaged in this common work to communicate upon subjects of importance, with a view to an interchange of ideas, and the establishment of unity of action in the various centres.

TERMS OF SUBSCRIPTION.

ONE YEAR'S SUBSCRIPTION	3s.	0d.
HALF ,, ,, ...	1s.	6d.
SINGLE COPY		3d.
POSTAGE MONTHLY EXTRA		1d.

Cheques and Post Office Orders to be made payable to
CHAPMAN & HALL, Limited.

THE FORTNIGHTLY REVIEW.

Edited by FRANK HARRIS.

THE FORTNIGHTLY REVIEW is published on the 1st of every month, and a Volume is completed every Six Months.

The following are among the Contributors :—

ADMIRAL LORD ALCESTER.
GRANT ALLEN.
SIR RUTHERFORD ALCOCK.
AUTHOR OF "GREATER BRITAIN."
PROFESSOR BAIN.
SIR SAMUEL BAKER.
PROFESSOR BEESLY.
PAUL BOURGET.
BARON GEORGE VON BUNSEN.
DR. BRIDGES.
HON. GEORGE C. BRODRICK.
JAMES BRYCE, M.P.
THOMAS BURT, M.P.
SIR GEORGE CAMPBELL, M.P.
THE EARL OF CARNARVON.
EMILIO CASTELAR.
RT. HON. J. CHAMBERLAIN, M.P.
PROFESSOR SIDNEY COLVIN.
THE EARL COMPTON.
MONTAGUE COOKSON, Q.C.
L. H. COURTNEY, M.P.
G. H. DARWIN.
SIR GEORGE W. DASENT.
PROFESSOR A. V. DICEY.
PROFESSOR DOWDEN.
RT. HON. M. E. GRANT DUFF.
RIGHT HON. H. FAWCETT, M.P.
ARCHDEACON FARRAR.
EDWARD A. FREEMAN.
J. A. FROUDE.
MRS. GARRET-ANDERSON.
J. W. L. GLAISHER, F.R.S.
SIR J. E. GORST, Q.C, M.P.
EDMUND GOSSE.
THOMAS HARE.
FREDERIC HARRISON.
ADMIRAL SIR G. P. HORNBY.
LORD HOUGHTON.
PROFESSOR HUXLEY.
PROFESSOR R. C. JEBB.
ANDREW LANG.
EMILE DE LAVELEYE.
T. E. CLIFFE LESLIE.
W. S. LILLY.
MARQUIS OF LORNE.

PIERRE LOTE.
SIR JOHN LUBBOCK, Bart., M.P.
THE EARL OF LYTTON.
SIR H. S. MAINE.
CARDINAL MANNING.
DR. MAUDSLEY.
PROFESSOR MAX MÜLLER.
GEORGE MEREDITH.
RT. HON. G. OSBORNE MORGAN, Q.C., M.P.
PROFESSOR HENRY MORLEY.
RT. HON. JOHN MORLEY, M.P.
WILLIAM MORRIS.
PROFESSOR H. N. MOSELEY.
F. W. H. MYERS.
F. W. NEWMAN.
PROFESSOR JOHN NICHOL.
W. G. PALGRAVE.
WALTER H. PATER.
RT. HON. LYON PLAYFAIR, M.P.
SIR HENRY POTTINGER, Bart.
PROFESSOR J. R. SEELEY.
LORD SHERBROOKE.
PROFESSOR SIDGWICK.
HERBERT SPENCER.
M. JULES SIMON. (Doctor L'Académie Française)
HON. E. L. STANLEY.
SIR J. FITZJAMESSTEPHEN, Q.C.
LESLIE STEPHEN.
J. HUTCHISON STIRLING.
A. C. SWINBURNE.
DR. VON SYBEL.
J. A. SYMONDS.
SIR THOMAS SYMONDS. (Admiral of the Fleet)
THE REV. EDWARD F. TALBOT (Warden of Keble College).
SIR RICHARD TEMPLE, Bart.
HON. LIONEL A. TOLLEMACHE.
H. D. TRAILL.
PROFESSOR TYNDALL.
A. J. WILSON.
GEN. VISCOUNT WOLSELEY.
THE EDITOR.

&c. &c. &c.

THE FORTNIGHTLY REVIEW *is published at* 2s. 6d.

CHAPMAN & HALL, LIMITED, 11, HENRIETTA STREET, COVENT GARDEN, W.C.

CHARLES DICKENS AND EVANS.]   [CRYSTAL PALACE PRESS.

CPSIA information can be obtained
at www.ICGtesting.com
Printed in the USA
BVHW03s1448070518
515500BV00026B/1402/P